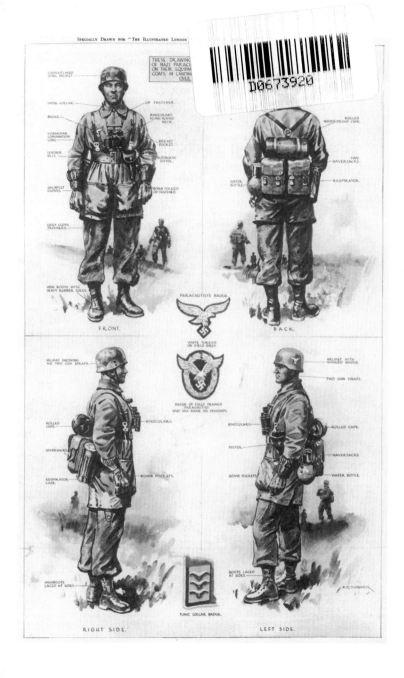

THESE DRAWINGS
OF NAZI PARAC[...]
ON THEIR EQUIPM[...]
COATS IN LANDIN[...]
OVER.

FRONT.

CAMOUFLAGED STEEL HELMET.
LOOSE COLLAR.
BADGE.
GABARDINE COMBINATION COAT.
LEATHER BELT.
GAUNTLET GLOVES.
GREY CLOTH TROUSERS.
HIGH BOOTS WITH HEAVY RUBBER SOLES.

ZIP FASTENER.
BINOCULARS SLUNG ROUND NECK.
BREAST POCKET.
AUTOMATIC PISTOL.
BOMB POCKETS ZIP FASTENED.

BACK.

ROLLED WATER-PROOF CAPE.
TWO HAVERSACKS.
RESPIRATOR.
WATER BOTTLE.

PARACHUTISTS BADGE

WHITE THREAD ON FIELD GREY

BADGE OF FULLY TRAINED PARACHUTIST WHO HAS MADE SIX DESCENTS.

RIGHT SIDE.

HELMET SHOWING THE TWO CHIN STRAPS.
ROLLED CAPE.
HAVERSACKS.
RESPIRATOR CASE.
HIGH BOOTS LACED AT SIDES.

BINOCULARS.
BOMB POCKETS.

TUNIC COLLAR BADGE.

LEFT SIDE.

HELMET WITH WINGED BADGE.
TWO CHIN STRAPS.
BINOCULARS.
PISTOL.
BOMB POCKETS.
ROLLED CAPE.
HAVERSACKS.
WATER BOTTLE.
BOOTS LACED AT SIDES.

C.E. TURNER

DEALING WITH THE
DIVE BOMBER AT
OSTERLEY PARK

MEMBERS OF THE HOME GUARD PRACTISING
RAPID RIFLE FIRE AGAINST A DIVING PLANE.

THE MODEL REPRESENTS A 50 ft. SPAN PLANE,
DIVING FROM A HEIGHT OF 1500 ft. THE TIME
TAKEN FOR THIS MODEL TO REACH THE BOTTOM OF
ITS WIRE RUNWAY IS ROUGHLY 3 SECONDS.

WHEN IT IS WITHIN 18 INCHES OF THE
GROUND IT SWOOPS UPWARDS IN A STEEP
CLIMB BARELY SKIMMING THE HEADS OF THE
FIRING PARTY.

THE MAXIMUM RATE OF FIRE HAS PROVED
TO BE THREE ROUNDS, THAT IS, TWO AS THE
MACHINE DESCENDS, AND ONE AS IT SOARS
UPWARDS TOWARDS THE TREE TOPS.

A MEDLEY OF BURSTING FIRE CRACKERS
ARE LET LOOSE FOR SOUND EFFECTS AND TO
DISCONCERT THE RIFLEMEN.

VARIOUS SHALLOW TRENCHES AFFORD A
VARIETY OF FIRING POSITIONS, AND THE WHOLE
CONTRIVANCE MAKES EXCELLENT PRACTICE
FOR QUICK AIMING AND LOADING.

- CUNRO -

THE BRITISH
HOME GUARD
POCKET-BOOK

(Sussex H.G.)

by

Brig.-Gen. A. F. U. GREEN, C.M.G., D.S.O., p.s.c.

(Formerly Volunteer, in the STORRINGTON Platoon,
W.S.H.G., now Commanding 4th Battalion, Sussex
Home Guard, and Training Advisor, Sussex Zone.)

Introduction by Brian Lavery

CONWAY

First printed	..	October, 1940
Second Impression	..	November, 1940
Third Impression	..	January, 1941
Fourth Impression	..	July, 1941
Fifth Impression	..	December, 1941
Sixth Impression	..	August, 1942
Second Edition	..	October, 1942

**In memory of Patrick Lavery, 1905–1980,
Dumbarton Home Guard, 1940–1944**

Introduction © Brian Lavery 2009
Volume © Conway 2009

This edition first published in 2009 by Conway
An imprint of Anova Books Ltd
10 Southcombe Street
London W14 0RA
www.conwaypublishing.com
www.anovabooks.com

Distributed in the U.S. and Canada by:
Sterling Publishing Co., Inc.
387 Park Avenue South
New York, NY 10016-8810

All rights reserved. No part of this publication may be reproduced, stored
in a retrieval system, or transmitted in any form or by any means electronic,
mechanical, photocopying, recording or otherwise, without the prior
permission of the copyright owner.

A CIP catalogue record for this book is available from the British Library.

ISBN 9781844861064

Printed and bound by WS Bookwell OY Ltd., Finland

To receive regular email updates on forthcoming Conway titles, email
conway@anovabooks.com with Conway Update in the subject field.

CONTENTS

FOREWORD
by
Colonel Ebenezer Pike, C.B.E., M.C.,
Zone Commander, Sussex H.G.

"Aim high and perchance ye may attain"
(The Late Field Marshal Earl Haig).

We Home Guards are now more than two years old. As Local Defence Volunteers we were in our infancy when the Sussex Home Guard Pocket Book was first published in 1940. We have since grown in stature and importance; His Majesty has become our Colonel in Chief; we have a form of compulsory service, yet our voluntary spirit easily absorbs all newcomers.

We are now well armed and equipped, and are rapidly reaching a satisfactory state of military efficiency.

We are proud of our Service and of our comradeship, and look forward to the time when, after the victory is won, we shall play our part in the regeneration of the Country.

The first edition of the West Sussex Home Guard Pocket Book has now reached a circulation of over 22,000. It has proved its high value both from training and operational points of view. Testimony as to its value has come from all parts of the country and in preparing this revised and enlarged Second Edition, my friend, General Green, has had in mind wider limits and to-day's conception of the role and duties of the Home Guard.

As for the First Edition, so with this one, I commend it to the serious study of all members of the Home Guard.

EBENEZER PIKE.

INTRODUCTORY NOTE (1940).

MOTTO: In war there are two kinds of men, the quick and the dead.
You be quick.

(1) This handbook is the result of my ransacking the dusty pigeon-holes of memory and the condensation of many books, official instructions and writings.

(2) The intention is to explain what we are for and how we are to do it.

(3) The spirit which should inspire the Home Guards in defending their country against invasion ought to be that exhibited by the Australians in the Great War, during 1917:

A machine gun post was found with all its defenders dead, and inside the post, fastened to the wall, were the following orders, in words which have become immortal:—

> (a) This position will be held, and the section will remain here until relieved.
>
> (b) The enemy cannot be allowed to interfere with this position.
>
> (c) If the section cannot remain here alive it will remain here dead, but in any case it will remain here.
>
> (d) Should any man through shell-shock or any cause attempt to surrender he will remain here dead.
>
> (e) Should all guns be blown up, the section will use Mills grenades and other novelties.
>
> (f) Finally, the position will be held as stated.

(4) It has been well said: "The ideal of every soldier is to make and keep himself fit for war, to obey orders promptly, intelligently and vigorously. Never, without orders, to abandon a position once occupied or won, to fight so long as he is physically capable of movement and to prefer death to surrender." The Home Guard are soldiers.

It is impossible to acknowledge all sources of information but thanks are due particularly to those whose names appear at the top of the sections they have contributed.

(5) I am also extremely grateful to Mr. E. A. Mitchell (of the *Worthing Gazette*), to whose professional help and energetic co-operation the quick production of this book is due.

(6) I wish to acknowledge the help and advice of Colonel Ebenezer Pike, M.C. Zone-Commander, W.S.H.G., and of Major H. Shiner,

D.S.O., M.C., his Staff Officer, also of Major J. W. Whitlock who has found time in his many activities, including those connected with the Sussex Zone Demonstration Unit, to carry this book through all its stages.

NOTE TO THE 5TH IMPRESSION, 1941.

I am grateful to the large number of readers of all ranks who have so generously expressed approval, and it may be of interest to know that General officers holding high commands can appreciate a colloquial way of talking shop as much as my comrades in the ranks.

In bringing the book up to date it may be observed that I have not included descriptions of the weapons, etc., which have been issued to us in growing numbers during recent months. This is because the W.O. are now in a position to issue admirable comprehensive manuals (and instructors!) with the weapons, whereas when the L.D.V. were formed we had to do the best we could with very scanty information.

My original aim was to give in compact form an outline of "most of the knowledge necessary for the Home Guard," and it is not loaded now with pages of detail which can be got straight from an officer or specialist or manual; in short, I have tried to preserve the original character of the book and some of that "Home Guard spirit" with which it has been credited, and which is not always to be found in manuals.

NOTE TO THE 2ND EDITION, 1942.

Contrary to the usual practice of paying for advice and not taking it, I am taking the gratuitous advice of high military and H.G. authorities and am altering the original H.G. Pocket Book as little as possible.

Much of it is old but, as has been pointed out, we are now getting many men into the Service who have not been through the mill in this war and to whom it may be helpful to give in compact form principles and details which, though available in official manuals and textbooks, are not always accessible to the Rank and File.

Nearly everything connected with the rifle or the B.A.R. or M.G. or any other H.G. weapon is fully described in official publications, or may be taught by the H.G. Training Officer or P.S.I. or other expert, so it may be thought that a book such as this is unnecessary. That is not so, let every H.G. study this (or some better) *vade mecum*, he will learn a lot, he may bump into some things he does not agree with—well, let him get doubtful points settled by an Instructor whom he trusts and who can turn up the official Instruction.

Suggestions and criticisms from my readers will be welcome. It may be worth recording that I have only received three criticisms since September, 1940. (1) "Put in more Fieldcraft." I answer that in the text. Fieldcraft and Battlecraft can only be taught by practical tough guys and not by me on paper. (2) One Platoon Commander thought it silly to refer to his men by the numbers by which they were "numbered off." He knew every man in his Platoon as Jones or Smith, or Bill or Joseph. But if Jones and Smith and Bill are casualties or lost and you have picked up stragglers, or supposing *you* are dead and some other man has taken charge who knows not Joseph. Surely it is better to get your men into action properly numbered off? Do it your own way, but, as an old gunner, I prefer to say, "Number one takes charge," rather than Serjeant Gubbins will assume control in the event of hypothetical eventualities necessitating the transfer of operational command. . . . (3) the third criticism was that there was no index. This has been remedied.

A lot of this book is out of date and gets more out of date every day. Battle-drill is to some extent replacing formal drill on the parade ground. Some day I hope to cut out pages and pages and to refer readers to official instructions: in the meantime, here is something for H.G. to read and digest in their spare time (if any).

A. F. U. G.

Storrington,
October, 1942.

INTRODUCTION

In the spring of 1940, as the British army retreated in France and the threat of a German invasion began to surface, the War Minister, Anthony Eden, addressed the nation by radio.

> We want large numbers of such men in Great Britain who are British subjects, between the ages of seventeen and sixty-five, to come forward now and offer their services in order to make assurance doubly sure. The name of the new force which is now to be raised will be the Local Defence Volunteers. The name describes its duties in three words. You will not be paid, but you will receive uniforms and will be armed. In order to volunteer, what you have to do is give your name at your local police station, and then, when we want you, we will let you know . . .

Even before Eden had finished speaking crowds were gathering outside police stations waiting to enlist, bewildering local constables who had not been briefed. The need for the new force became more urgent in the next few weeks as the British army was brought home from Dunkirk defeated and without equipment and the apparently invincible forces of Nazi Germany massed on the other side of the English Channel. The Local Defence Volunteers (soon to be renamed the Home Guard) were a national phenomenon. Basil Boothroyd of *Punch* magazine wrote,

> For some reason or other the press has taken us to its fickle heart. We take precedence over the R.A.F., Mr Churchill and Gracie Fields. We appear in every other headline. The penny papers have special articles telling us how to take cover behind trees and how deep we ought to dig our trenches. *The Times* has light leaders about our neckties and whole columns of correspondence about whether we're worth one-and-sixpence a night or not.[1]

The idea of a force of volunteers for the defence against invasion was not a new one, and during the scare of 1803–5 when the enemy was Napoleon rather than Hitler, there had been almost equal enthusiasm. Then the War Office had envisaged warfare by small groups of men who knew the country and one another – '. . . no Company should be formed of a greater

[1] *Punch*, 4 September 1940, p. 244

Number of People than what are already known to each other, to act under Leaders known to each Individual, and whose Intelligence and Prudence all have equal Confidence.'

It was believed that the French invasion could not be reinforced by sea, therefore, '. . . whilst our own Army becomes every Day more powerful, several Causes must operate towards the Diminution of his [the enemy's] original Numbers. His Losses from partial Engagements, constant Fatigue, and precarious Sustenance, are in themselves sufficient to decide his fate, independent of any decisive Action being fought, which may annihilate his Army at one Blow.' In attacking the enemy:

> From the first Moment of a Landing being made, the great Object of the Irregular Troops must be to *Harass, Alarm* and *Fatigue* an Enemy. Nothing can more effectually contribute to this Object than the Operations of small Bodies of Men well acquainted with the Country, who will approach and fire upon the Advanced Posts of his Army, without ever engaging in serious Action, or hazarding themselves, in any situation where their natural Intelligence and Watchfulness does not ensure the Danger of being cut off. So long as they are *watchful* to this Point, it must be evident, that with the Country open in their Rear, and with the Advantage of knowing all the Avenues and Roads, having an Enemy who is ignorant of them; and who can likewise have but a small proportion if any Cavalry; that nothing can expose them to any other Danger than what their own Energy and Courage had determine them to face.[2]

This was a remarkable description of guerrilla warfare as it would soon be seen in Spain against the French.

In 1940, as in 1803, West Sussex, with its beaches less than 60 miles from the French coast, was one of the most vulnerable areas to invasion and the Local Defence Volunteers (LDV) there had attracted 1500 volunteers within four days of the announcement of the force on 20 May. A company was formed in the seaside resort of Worthing under Lt-Col. M. Kent, with platoons in the town and in outlying villages. Two local benefactors offered £1000 each for arms and equipment, and boys were seen playing at LDVs instead of soldiers. Members of Air Raid

[2] National Archives, WO 30/70

Precautions (ARP) were found to be resigning from their unpopular duties in enforcing the blackout to join the volunteers, which seemed much more relevant in the circumstances. Later a theatre in Worthing was taken over as headquarters and a canteen was set up. A few local Fascist supporters were arrested and the professional at a local golf club used his LDV training to arrest a man who broke into the clubhouse, but there was no real sign of the notorious 'fifth column' which was believed to have helped the Germans in the Low Countries and France.[3]

Among those who came forward was a 61-year-old, sciatica-ridden, retired Brigadier-General. Arthur Frank Umfreville Green lived in the village of West Chiltington a few miles away. Born in Chatham to a family of bankers, he was educated at Haileybury School where he found his teachers, with one exception, 'did not even know what teaching meant.'[4] He did, however, learn to draw well before he was sent to 'Jimmy's', a well-known 'crammer', which prepared boys for service entrance examinations. He entered the Royal Military Academy at Woolwich and developed another great talent, shooting, before being commissioned as an artillery officer in 1897. He had a remarkable military career, seeing action in the South African War (1899–1902) and at the First Battle of Ypres in 1914. By 1916 he had risen to become Quartermaster-General of XI Corps, administering the needs of up to 120,000 men. After the war he was Chief of Staff to the Armistice Commission and then with the government of Malta until 1924. He moved to Chiltington around 1934 when he married Mrs Annie Livingstone, a widow with one son. As war approached he considered joining the expanding Territorial Army but ruled it out on health grounds, and his applications for jobs with the War Office only got 'the stereotyped reply'. He was working in the local ARP control room when the call came and he volunteered for the Storrington Platoon of the LDV.

The village of Storrington is eight miles from the south coast of England, just north of Worthing but protected by the chalk hills of the South Downs. Its Home Guard platoon was one of the first to be formed, though according to the local newspapers the people seemed more worried about the lack of protection during air raids, than the threat of invasion. The Home Guard took over an evacuated monastery as its headquarters and began to patrol the Downs against paratroopers, as well as guarding a rail tunnel for possible saboteurs. The men were allowed to

[3] Local papers, *Worthing Herald* and *Worthing Gazette,* passim
[4] A. F. U. Green, *Evening Tattoo*, London, 1941, p. 22

practise occasionally on ranges operated by Canadian troops stationed nearby, and sometimes the units exercised together.[5]

Green joined rather late in the day on 15 June, more than three weeks after the LDV was formed, but his qualifications would naturally fit him for command. The other officers of the Worthing Company included retired captains and majors, all junior to him. His sciatica had been cured but he still considered himself very unfit and wrote, 'I refused any command because I knew I was not fit enough to do the walking necessary.'[6] The early Home Guard was an egalitarian force which did not use conventional military ranks. According to the Local Defence Volunteers Instruction No. 6 of July 1940:

> For general administration L.D.V.s are organised into battalion units. A battalion may consist of 4 companies each of 4 platoons. A platoon has 4 sections each of approximately 24 men. The number of sub-units in a battalion, company, etc., vary however, to meet local circumstances. The commanders are designated battalion, company, platoon commanders and wear 3, 2 and 1 stripes respectively on their shoulder straps. Section Commanders wears [sic] 3 chevrons (serjeant's pattern) on their left arm. All ranks wear the L.D.V. arm band on the right arm.

A detachment in any locality may therefore be a section, platoon, company or, in exceptional circumstances, a battalion under its commander.[7]

Green fitted in well with this organisation and wrote, 'I was a young brigadier-general nearly twenty-five years ago, and was proud of it. I am a damned sight prouder to be an old volunteer today and to show respect to those put in authority over me . . .'[8] He took on the job of musketry instructor, as well as searching for much needed weapons and advising the commanders of other units.

> My job is a funny one – I sort of invented it myself as I went on. Apart from musketry, which I still keep on, it is my duty to scour the county for the Zone Commander and to visit anybody I like and see what their troubles and difficulties are and try to help them find a remedy.

[5] *Storrington at War*, pp 81-3, 88, *Sussex Home Guard*, pp 16, 68-9
[6] *Tattoo*, p. 249
[7] National Archives, WO 199/872B
[8] *Tattoo*, p. 252-53

It is a delightful job – I meet Battalion commanders on as friendly terms as do the rank and file and am glad to have evidence that some of my efforts produce results.[9]

Green was already a very experienced writer. In South Africa he 'became a prolific contributor to local papers and published every week drawings and cartoons, articles, stories, and (may I be forgiven!) poetry.'[10] In 1904–5 he published the novels *As Down of Thistle* and *The Countermine* under the pseudonym of Arthur Wenlock, followed by the more practical *Landscape Sketching for Military Purposes* under his own name in 1908. He made contributions to the *United Services Magazine*, and as an aide to the Governor of Gibraltar just before the First World War he edited a local newspaper.

HOW TO FIRE A RIFLE

In 1940 the Home Guard was issued with American P17, 'Springfield' or Canadian 'Ross' rifles instead of the more popular British Lee-Enfield but there was no instruction book for them. Green used his skill in writing and musketry to produce a short handbook for distribution by Zone Headquarters, and this led to the present volume. 'Of course I have called down Nemesis on my own head – and have been given the task of compiling a hand-book of simple instructions on all the different duties of the Home Guard – a big task, which I shall try my best to boil down to the lowest terms'[11] At the same time he was completing his autobiography, *Evening Tattoo*, which was 'racing neck and neck for the bookstalls' with the *Home Guard Pocket Book*. Both were in print by the beginning of 1941.

Top: Position of elbows on the ground.

Bottom: Position of body. Both feet should be spread at this angle with heels on the ground.

Green considered himself something of a humorist. 'I still have a letter from Rudyard Kipling congratulating me on one of my effusions which, as a matter of fact, was intended to be a parody of his work.'[12] He submitted

[9] *Tattoo*, p. 249
[10] *Tattoo*, p. 26
[11] *Tattoo*, p. 250
[12] *Tattoo*, p. 26

cartoons to *Punch* magazine, the centrepiece of British humour of the day. Some of his jokes need explanation today and for the one on page 21 the reader needs to know that a 'general' could also mean a maid-of-all-work. Others, for example on page 77 and page 155, would be considered offensive today. They might have gone down well with the 'brutal and licentious soldiers' he mentioned ironically on page 155, but the more staid and conventional audience of the West Sussex Home Guard might well have considered them rather *risqué*. The reader today has to judge whether they succeed in lightening a technical manual, or detract from its messages.

The *Home Guard Pocket Book* was by no means the only work on part-time military service to be published during the war. At least 130 books with Home Guard in the title were out before the force was disbanded in 1944. Paper rationing restricted the activities of publishers very severely, but clearly this was an exception. There were several general handbooks by the journalist John Brophy. Tom Wintringham, a former communist and leader of the British Battalion of the International Brigades in the Spanish Civil War, advocated people's war in *The Home Guard Can Fight.* There were many more specialised manuals on subjects such as night fighting, first aid, organising an exercise, unarmed action, administration, legal rights and powers, grenades, rifles, map reading, fieldcraft, camouflage, signalling, and *Total War Training for Home Guard Officers and N.C.O.s.*

Basil Boothroyd published *Home Guard Goings On* from *Punch* in 1941, and there was a book of cartoons, *Laughs with the Home Guard,* edited by Samuel Thomas. Compton Mackenzie published his novel *Keep the Home Guard Turning* in 1943. It would form the basis for his much more famous *Whisky Galore.* A book of Home Guard poetry was published by A. H. Watkins; there were marches composed by W. J. Dutoit and Wilfred Basford and a play, *According to Plan,* by Lawrence du Garde Peach. There was a mystery, *Murder in the Home Guard,* by the feminist writer Ruth Adam and even a children's book, *Hare Joins the Home Guard,* by Alison Uttley. Some units produced their own magazines, including *The Home Guardian* by the 2nd Edinburgh Battalion and *The Night-Hawk* by the 14th Sussex Battalion in Hove. The first general history of the force was published by Charles Graves in 1943, while individual units were publishing their own by 1944.

Not all the Home Guard books lived up to their titles. *Home Guard Training* by Lt-Col. J. H. Levey was produced very quickly in 1940, but a large proportion of its 48 pages were devoted to foot drill and rather obscure subjects such as 'Piling and Unpiling Arms'. *The Home Guard Encyclopedia* by Andrew G. Elliot and others was far short of encyclopaedic. It was only 128 pages long and contained unbelievably optimistic diagrams of the Home Guard 'smashing out of the jaws of death' and taking on enemy forces including tanks. The War Office tended to be sceptical of their value and pointed out that , '. . . no pamphlet or document on training has the stamp of official authority unless it has been submitted to the Director of Military Training and received his approval.'[13] Green's book did eventually attain this status. Compared with many others, his effort was realistic, practical and generally accessible.

By the time Green produced his second edition in 1942, the Home Guard had changed. Uniforms were issued late in 1940, initially in the form of denim overalls. According to Basil Boothroyd,

> The evening's parade was one of mingled embarrassment and pride. We were embarrassed because the little boys ran after us, delightedly reading the sizes from the tickets on our backs and our trousers, and expressing pardonable surprise that Mr. King, at four feet ten, wore size nine-and-a-half, while Mr. Benn the butcher (six feet tall and practically square) had chosen size three, medium. . . . Yet we were proud, though none of us would perhaps have admitted it; for we were wearing the King's uniform, even if it did fit our functions rather than our physique.[14]

These were eventually replaced by standard army khaki battledress. At the same time the rank structure became more similar to that of the army, with colonels, majors, captains and corporals, for example.

As Green wrote and many others agreed, 'The Platoon is the essential unit in the Home Guard and the Platoon area is the essential administrative subdivision of the county.'[15] 'Contrary to what happens in mobile armies, the Home Guard is never intended to operate in Battalions or Companies manoeuvring in a formed body; nor, as a general rule, is it likely that anything larger than a Platoon will act as a formed body for a specific operation.'[16] The Home Guard reflected the rest of the

---

[13] WO 199/872B

[14] *Punch*, 4 December 1940, p. 456

population, so the great bulk of it lived in the towns, and large numbers of others were in factory units largely for the defence of their own workplaces. But it was generally agreed that the real role of the Home Guard was in the country, where the people had an almost mystical bond with the land they were defending. As the writer and broadcaster J. B. Priestley put it on the radio the day after Green joined,

> Ours is a small and scattered village, but we'd had a fine response to the call for volunteers; practically every able-bodied man in the place takes his turn. . . . I think the countryman knows, without being told, that we hold our lives here, as we hold our farms, upon certain terms. One of these terms is that while wars still continue, while one nation is ready to hurl its armed men at another, you must necessarily stand up and fight for your own. . . . I felt too up there a powerful and rewarding sense of community; and with it too a feeling of deep continuity. There we were, ploughman and parson, shepherd and clerk, turning out at night, as our forefathers had often done before us, to keep watch and ward over the sleeping English hills.[17]

Green's book reflects this, and most of his tactics are based on defending the country or small villages rather than street fighting in cities and towns where the great majority of Home Guard members lived, and he says nothing about factory defence which was regarded as a primary role in the early days. He is generally a conservative tactician, and he gives no indication of the great debate within the Home Guard during 1940. Tom Wintringham, a former communist, wanted them to be a people's army, trained mainly in guerrilla warfare and with a minimum of formal drill and discipline. This idea gained a good deal of momentum in the early days, as Wintringham had the support of the wealthy publisher Edward Hulton to set up a training school at Osterley Park near London. George Orwell, a sergeant in a London unit, was characteristically sceptical about the possibilities and wrote, 'The Home Guard swells to a million men in a few weeks, and is deliberately organised in such a way that only people with private incomes can hold positions of command.' It was,

[15] A. F. U. Green, *Home Guard Pocket Book*, p. 16
[16] A. F. U. Green, *Home Guard Pocket Book*, p. 12
[17] J. B. Priestley, *All England Listened*, pp 14-8

> . . . the most anti-Fascist body existing in England at this moment, and at the same time is an astonishing phenomenon, a sort of people's army officered by Blimps. The rank and file are predominantly working class, with a strong middle-class seasoning, but practically all the commands are held by wealthy elderly men, a lot of whom are utterly incompetent.

In any case, the War Office had largely sidestepped the issue by early 1941, by setting up its own training schools.

Green does not deal with another issue which affected the Home Guard. Women's Home Defence was set up in December 1940 and had the active support of a well-known Labour MP, Dr Edith Summerskill. Its aim was,

> To train every woman in the Country to be of the maximum use in the event of an invasion. This does not mean that they will be issued with rifles – the combatant services must have the first call on all weapons – but it is essential that they shall be proficient in certain forms of defence.

This found no support in the government, though women's auxiliary units were formed to help with the paperwork and in 1942 Mrs H. C. I. Gwynne-Vaughan published a booklet on *Military Correspondence for Volunteers*. Thousands of other women performed traditional roles as wives and mothers, repairing uniforms or providing sandwiches for exercises.

For most people, the Home Guard was first and foremost a defence against German paratroops, which had surprised the world by their novelty during the recent campaign in the Netherlands and Belgium. Indeed the press soon bestowed the nickname 'parashots' or 'parashooters' on the volunteers, and this was taken up by the *Worthing Gazette* as early as 22 May 1940. But Green devotes comparatively little attention to this issue, only two short paragraphs on page 112. Perhaps he felt there was no need to supplement LDV Training Instruction No. 3 of June 1940, which devoted eight pages to the subject; or perhaps he was simply thinking more of the old-fashioned war he knew on the Western Front. But in a sense he was right to do so; the German paratroops were less efficient and infinitely less ubiquitous than the public tended to believe in 1940.

" I think it's silly the way you try to find a perfectly natural explanation for every thing I want to report."

Illustration from *Punch*, 11 September 1940.

Green is equally sanguine about tanks and sums them up in a single phrase – 'The tank is a terror at 200 yards – it is a poor blind beggar when you can touch it.'[18] This agrees with the Wintringham school of warfare;

> If the question is asked about any sort of tank, "What is its weakest point?" the answer that should be given is always "The minds of the men inside it." They are men like ourselves, subject to fear and fatigue, they are half-stifled, they cannot see well, hostility is all round them. Anything new or strange within their field of vision checks them or spurs them to a mad rush. They cannot drive their desperately uncomfortable vehicle continuously at high speeds. They can be fought at any time, when moving fast or when moving slowly; when at rest they should be hunted. A tank at rest is a target for men stalking it; a tank moving is something to be trapped and ambushed.[19]

Green is rather ambiguous about the use of the bayonet, which was at least as useful a tool as a weapon, for opening doors and dealing with other obstacles.

[18] A. F. U. Green, *Home Guard Pocket Book*, p. 95
[19] Tom Wintringham, *The Home Guard Can Fight*, p. 15

The third factor in German success was the dive bomber, and again Green is sanguine – 'In dive bombing you must carry on as if there was no dive bombing going on – it is very frightening but nothing like as dangerous as it sounds. If it makes you get your head under cover it will have served its purpose – do not put your head down.'[20]

Though Green was apparently lacking any personal ambition within the Home Guard, and accepted demotion to private in 1943, he had high hopes for the body he had joined. As early as 1940 he dreamed of a force 'ready now to shoulder the principal burden of the land defence of these Islands' so that the regulars could concentrate on campaigns overseas. This was a long way from fruition even in 1942 when the invasion threat was much reduced and the force had been organised on strict military lines. Green envisaged new terms of recruitment so that men were not bound to their local area, and a certain amount of road transport would be provided. But would such a force ever be able to concentrate against a major attack, or to launch a counter attack on a national rather than a local scale? It was all very different from the local platoon where everyone knew everyone else, and was familiar with the countryside he was operating in. The change that Green envisaged would have created a very different force, and it might have been better to create a new one, or revive the old functions of the Territorial Army.

The village of Storrington did indeed feature in the German invasion plan. According to the final version, one of four landings would take place between Brighton and Eastbourne and some of the units would swing left to run parallel to the South Downs with a view to cutting off the West Country. Storrington would have been directly in the way of this. Of course the invasion was never launched, and probably never could have been as the German plans for transporting an army across the channel were completely impracticable.[21] We will never really know how well the Home Guard would have fought, but Green gives a clue to his own attitude when he writes that the less fit men (presumably including himself) would 'sit on their backsides and die, reluctantly but venomously'.[22]

BRIAN LAVERY

---

[20] A.F.U. Green, *Home Guard Pocket Book*, p. 95
[21] Peter Schenk, *The Invasion of England 1940*, London, 1990, passim
[22] A. F. U. Green, *Home Guard Pocket Book*, p. 15

CHAPTER I.
(A) Role. (B) Object. (C) Notes on Discipline.

(A) ROLE OF THE HOME GUARD.

(1) Observation and prompt correct reporting of information.

(2) Delaying and obstructing the enemy by any means in their power.

(3) Protection of vulnerable and key points such as factories, railways, bridges, Post Office systems, etc.

(4) Keeping a check on subversive activities.

(5) Co-operation with Civil Defence Services.

(6) Acting as guides to the Military.

(7) Controlling the movement and helping to maintain the morale of the civil population.

(B) THE OBJECT OF THE HOME GUARD.

(1) **The object of the Home Guard** is to augment the local defences of Great Britain by helping to localise enemy action and to hold up and harass parachutists until stronger forces arrive, also to impede hostile forces in every way as well as give timely information of enemy movement.

(2) As I see it, our only excuse for existence is to look out for Germans and to help the military to kill them or—better still—kill them ourselves.

(3) It is essential that in our organisation and training there shall be sufficient elasticity to enable a Home Guard unit to adapt itself to the needs of the moment and even to abandon all ideas of defence, and to **attack**.

(4) Home Guards are intended to take the place of, or help, the military in the defence of the locality to which they belong, and not on expeditions away from home. They may on occasion best help the military by acting as guides in the area they know rather than by fighting or sticking to their ordinary duties.

(C) NOTES ON DISCIPLINE, DRILL AND RANK.

(1) It is not intended that the Home Guard shall be made into Regulars: it is therefore sometimes thought they can do without discipline or with a sort of lax control under which each man can do more or less as he pleases—there is no greater or more dangerous fallacy.

(2) **Discipline** does not consist merely in smartness on parade—it consists in all working as a team and obeying a permanent or temporary **Leader** promptly, vigorously and intelligently—like a member of a team on the football field, or of a gang on the roads or in a workshop or a business.

The foundation of efficiency lies in discipline which, firstly, make us work together under leadership; secondly, makes us do the work according to a method thought out by experts; and, thirdly, establishes a system in which we do the job in accordance with the intention of our Commander.

It involves sacrifice of self-interests for the welfare of the whole.

(3) **Drill** is the orderly execution of tasks, actions or movements required of us by the Commander in accordance with clear rules which have been practised until our action is almost automatic. In short, if we are prepared to accept **discipline** under appointed Leaders, **drill** is the stuff to make it practicable for us to do what they say.

(4) It is no good saying "I will do what I am told" unless we know how to do it and have tried it out and are sure that we **can** do it. Even that is not enough, we must be sure that we can do it in the right way. The mounting of rails on a road-block is an admirable example of one form of drill required by H.G.

(5) In our history there are instances of rabbles without discipline and drill who did well in action, there are examples of highly trained regiments who were useless in battle, but, speaking generally—the fact sticks out a mile—those who fight best are those whose discipline and drill have been sedulously fostered.

(6) **Rank.** We are all H.G. with the honour, privilege and duty of enrolling as a Volunteer with the equivalent rank of Private. Those who are appointed to be Commanders or Leaders must take charge of those under them and require of them that they do what they are told. Any man so appointed—regardless of his previous rank or position—must be looked upon as the Boss, and each of us must serve any such man of any previous rank whatsoever with all the loyalty and energy of which we are capable.

Conflicting instructions about badges of rank and uniform created a problem which worried the H.G. from top to bottom. Are we to salute or not? Whom shall we salute? If, for example, a tradesman with no military prestige, except that he was a Captain in the last war, has in his unit an Admiral and a couple of Generals, the question they ask is "Who salutes whom?"

(7) My answer is clear:—"If I am a Volunteer in a section or a patrol commanded by a General or a Blacksmith or my own Gardener, I do what he orders to the best of my ability. And on parade I salute him."

If I am appointed to take charge of some particular job, all men working on that job have got to do what I order—whether they are Generals or Gardeners. And I do not require any of them to salute if they do not wish to. When the job is finished I revert to the ranks and will salute anyone who wants it, and I "muck in" with the others in the ranks whether they are Parsons or Publicans.

(8) **Badges of Rank.** This acute problem has now been solved. Rank has been given to officers, warrant officers and N.C.O.s in the Home Guard, with the appropriate badges, and we are in line with the Regular Services.

(9) Still we are not in many classes—only one class, or No Class.

"Darling!—My father was a General."—"How marvellous. Darling!—that seems to level us up somehow—so was my mother."

(10) **Duds, Dead-Weight and Passengers**—are they of any use to H.G.? What are we to do with malcontents and subversive individuals, or lazy and inefficient men? The answer is easy. As Mr. Middleton teaches us to prune roses, so can we prune our duds. "Ruthlessly" is the operative word. We are at war and there is no time to spare. If you see dead wood or anything unhealthy—cut it out. The chief trouble is the question whether there is new growth to replace it. This is the formula:

If your resources are rich, cut out every dud and burn it.

If your resources are poor, cut out the duds but don't burn them until it's clear they are useless in any capacity.

If your resources are "nil" give the young growth every chance and keep your duds, on the chance of their being some use in some other capacity.

(11) **Loyalty.** This word is so old-fashioned as to be almost indecent. Loyalty operates not only upwards to "God Save the King," but also downwards to the humblest of those under us and to our pals and neighbours. Whether it is old-fashioned or not, loyalty is an essential ingredient which with Discipline, Drill and Training, helps to make us fit for Service, which is better than fit for the scrap-heap.

(A) HIGHER ORGANISATION.

(1) **Higher Organisation.** It is not necessary yet to go into the whole complex subject of how the country is organised as a whole and how the H.G., the Military Authorities, the Civil Authorities and the Civil Defence services are dovetailed. This will be studied in greater detail later.

(2) It is sufficient to know that corresponding with (say) a County, a H.G. Zone has been formed. The Zone is divided into areas and the H.G. in each area form a Battalion. Similarly the Battalion is subdivided into Companies, Platoons, Sections, Sub-sections and smaller units called 'patrols,' etc.

Each of these is definitely a territorial unit in the literal sense. They live, train and operate in the immediate neighbourhood of their own homes.

(3) Contrary to what happens in mobile armies, the Home Guard is never intended to operate as Battalions or Companies manœuvring as a formed body; nor, as a general rule, is it likely that anything larger than a Platoon will act as a formed body for a specific operation. Generally, within a Platoon area, the duties are divided up between smaller bodies in such a way that each seems almost independent though, in fact, all the posts and localities occupied together build up a large scale scheme of Defence which has been elaborated by the Military Authorities.

(4) It is enough for the individual Home Guard to know generally what the Battalion he belongs to is doing and to know very thoroughly all about his Platoon and Platoon Area.

(B) THE BATTALION.

As shown in a later chapter on "Co-operation," the H.G. organization was born and has developed in an odd way, from the military point of view. Usually, Higher Authority says "Let there be a Battalion (or a Division, or an Army, or whatever is required)," and an "Establishment" is approved. This "Establishment" is a sort of blue-print of the machine to be created. It defines the elements of which the unit or formation should consist—the internal organization, i.e., H.Q., and whatever is required to make that H.Q. a functioning body, and so many sub-units of a certain approved structure each sub-divided in a specified way. That is the framework.

The numbers required to make of that unit an efficient force are also defined for each sub-unit and for H.Q.

When the "Establishment" has been clearly laid down on paper, the next step is to clothe that skeleton with flesh. Men are recruited by, or enrolled in, or drafted to, the embryo unit.

The numbers of men in that unit at any time constitute the "strength" of that unit. That is to say, during the formation of a unit with an invariable "Establishment" of 1,000 the "strength" will vary from day to day—it may be one day 15, next day 150, next week 750, and so on until 1,000 men are in that unit. The unit is then "up to Establishment"—if more men are enrolled it is "over Establishment."

I want now to emphasize the importance of differentiating clearly between "Establishment" and "strength." This is not pedantic—the words are continuously used wrongly in the Press and even by Secretaries of State, and if they are used wrongly, confusion is inevitable.

"The Battalion is up to strength" means nothing at all. If the strength of the Battalion is as laid down, then the Battalion is "up to "Establishment."

Now, the "Establishment" lays down for a Battalion so many Companies. Each Company is to be organized in such and such a way and to consist of so many Platoons. Each Platoon is to be sub-divided into Sections of a specified structure.

The "Establishment" also defines how weapons and equipment are allotted to the several sub-units or at least what are the weapons and equipment each is entitled to if up to "Establishment."

The ideal for that Battalion Commander, therefore, is to get casualties and wastage replaced so that always he shall have in his Battalion the number and resources laid down for him in his "Establishment."

In the H.G. it is all different, and must remain different for all time, owing to the entirely different conditions of service.

Every Battalion, Company and Platoon must be treated on its own intrinsic merits and two neighbouring units may of necessity be quite dissimilar.

This has always been recognized and that recognition is proved by the fact that we have never had an "Establishment" laid down. I think I am right in saying that at Battalion H.Q., a certain number of officers and other ranks are approved, at Company and Platoon H.Q. there is a Commanding Officer and Second in Command, and there are a few other duties to which W.O.'s and N.C.O.'s may be appointed with appropriate H.G. rank, but beyond that there is no "Establishment" of any kind whatsoever.

The manner of the birth of H.G. Battalions was something like this (I am only quoting a typical case so am in danger of being contradicted by every Commanding Officer):—

Disregarding ancient history, during which the sub-units were renamed—e.g., Platoon becoming Company, certain populous centres were obviously cut out to produce a Battalion. Some villages and small towns were good for a Company or Platoon, according to their potential man power.

We therefore find Battalions composed of a compact body of men who can be organized, trained and fought as one unit—or we find a town producing the best part of a Battalion, supplemented by satellite villages, each of which can produce a Company or a Platoon. For purposes of administration, such a Battalion is quite reasonable, though it may never fight as a Battalion. Again, we may find a Battalion which consists of entirely separated geographical localities each supporting a Company—such a Battalion must be considered as an administrative and training collection of companies which each have an independent operational role and which cannot be fought as a Battalion.

Each Company, in its turn, may have widely scattered Platoons, each with a separate operational role.

That is the picture of things as they are and it is clear that a stereotyped "Establishment" is out of the question.

The great variety of organizations is largely due to the different "potential" and circumstances in urban and truly rural districts.

Now take a typical rural Platoon.

When the H.G. were formed, a certain village produced anything from 25 to 100 men. These had obviously to be formed into a Company or Platoon. They had to be embraced in the general organization of a Battalion even though their operational role might lie outside the general role of the parent Battalion.

This particular village produced (say) 50 men. They had few or no weapons and were, for purposes of drill and training, merely 50 men who fell in on parade in an old-fashioned line.

By degrees more weapons were provided, but they were still just a row of men with a heterogeneous collection of arms—called a "Platoon" but having no real Platoon organization.

And then came the great awakening and it was realized that though we had no "Establishment" we had to carve out our own organization, and thus you will find all over the country Platoons with a well-thought-out organization into Sections, sometimes according to numbers, sometimes according to functions, and two neighbouring Platoons are not necessarily alike.

To-day, we have many obstacles to finality in organization.

One is the fluctuation in strength. We lose more by being called up than we gain by enrolment. Then, on compulsion being introduced, our numbers begin to rise. If the old Platoon of 50 increases to 100, should it be divided into two Platoons or what? It is sometimes thought that about 50 is ideal. But supposing you haven't got the Officers and N.C.O.'s to command two Platoons?

Another is the difficulty in reconciling the ideal of 50 for a Platoon with 10 or 12 for a Section.

Yet another is the need to embody our teams for special weapons such as M.G.'s, Northovers and Spigot Mortars, either as specialist Sections or sub-units.

And one more is that all H.G. are not equally active, tough and fit. Are we to clog the active H.G. wheels blessed with the oil of youth by the stickiness of physical disability?—In the H.G. the spirit is willing but the flesh is sometimes weak, or, as the old Professor said: "The ghost is willing, but the meat is feeble."

Here is my solution in general terms:—The Platoon consists of men of all categories. Some are fit and know everything, some are fit and know nothing. Many know a lot but are only fit for sedentary work. We have all sorts.

Very good—under the modern conditions of Battle Drill, we must have Sections (10 to 12 men) fit for any kind of military duty. We must also have Sections of men, not so fit; Sections which specialize in team weapons; Sections organized, armed and equipped like a Battle Drill Section in the Regular Army; some Sections which can only sit on their backsides and shoot and die, reluctantly but venomously.

The Company Commander has got to size his men up, weigh their individual capabilities and break up his Company into Platoons and his Platoons into Sections—not one of which need be identical with its neighbour.

Many years ago, a military expert was asked to write a short memorandum on the organization of the Army. He wrote: "The Army has no organization," and asked if that was short enough. To-day, it is for each H.G. Company and Platoon Commander to work out his own salvation and his improvised organization will only be proved to be good or bad when he tests it against the boche.

Another complication in the H.G. is the division of men into two categories called List (i) and List (ii).

List (i) are men who are supposed to be immediately available on "Action Stations"; List (ii) are men who, by reason of over-riding civil duties are not expected to be available for military duty until they are released from their work of national importance.

As a matter of fact, some List (i) men will not be immediately available, they may be cowmen or technicians or employees of some industrial concern. On the other hand, some List (ii) men may, quite unexpectedly, turn up. We must, therefore, reckon on a number of definitely List (i) and a number of definitely List (ii) and between these two categories are a large number of men who may or may not be immediately available.

The Company or Platoon Commander must, therefore, so organize his command that he has immediately available for his sections the men he knows will be there. He must also arrange to fit into their places the "perhapsers" and the men he knows will *not* be there when the flag falls.

It is for his consideration whether he will not be well advised to have a pool of the possibles and also some complete Sections of improbables who may form a valuable "first reinforcement."

To sum up the Battalion organization:—There must be an efficient Battalion H.Q. This is the brain and directing force in the Battalion. Each Company must have a Commander with appropriate staff. Each Company must be organized in Platoons, in each of which is a Commander (relieved of all "bumph"), whose duty is to organize *NOW* his Sections and command them in action; some of these Sections will be 100 per cent. active, some will be less active but none the less *real*. Each Section should be quite clear as to its role, which may be offensive, defensive, static or routine drudgery, commonly called "administrative."

(C) THE PLATOON.

(1) The Platoon is the essential unit in the Home Guard organisation and the Platoon Area is the essential administrative subdivision of the County. In the Platoon Area should be always—during hours of duty or on emergency—an "inlying picquet" of 1 and 3, or 1 and 6, or as many as the numbers available will permit, subject to the general rule that no man should be "on duty" more than one night in five (or, better still, one night in seven) and that the winter hours of duty are from 9 p.m. to 5 a.m.

This inlying picquet should be, for preference, at Platoon H.Q. The ideal arrangement, where possible, is to have H.Q., armoury, recreation room and observation post or strong point at one and the same place.

Every man, woman and child in the area should know where this post is and should be ready at any time to take information there or to co-operate with the men of the Platoon.

As, under the Territorial System, Regiments were identified with Counties, so, in the H.G., should Platoons be identified with their area (parish, or whatever it may be). Equally, H.G. Battalions should be proud of their connection with the County Regiment.

CHAPTER III.
(A) Training—General. (B) Leadership. (C) Orders.

(A) TRAINING.

(1) **Training** is not an end in itself but a means to an end. Its object is to enable a man to kill an enemy, or to help indirectly in the success of an operation, or to perform a service to his country where he could not have done without training.

(2) Training is (a) individual, and (b) collective. Some men want a lot of individual attention, others can go on to parade with a formed body very quickly. Instructors must study each man and try to get inside his head. The day of the bullying drill-sergeant is over. To-day, it is the Instructor who knows his job and understands men who can prepare Volunteers for their task.

(3) **Drill** is the basis of training but must not be worshipped as a fetish. Drill is necessary in every single operation, from a pitched battle down to firing one round from a rifle; we only want a little of it but that little must be good.

(4) The first stage in drill consists in standing still, turning right, left or about, moving to a flank in threes, keeping step, wheeling and halting, covering off and dressing. The idea of this is to get men used to doing things together intelligently instead of barging about like a football crowd.

Make a point at this elementary stage of always numbering off the squad and insist on the men knowing their own number. Action then becomes automatic if (for example) on patrol the leader suddenly orders "Numbers one, two and three line that ditch—number three take charge." How different to the slipshod way: "Hullo!—let's see, I want three of you—you, what's your name? Oh yes, and you too,—no, you're too fat. Off you go and line that blinkin' ditch. What's that? Who's in charge? Oh, we don't want nobody in charge when its only three men—corluvaduck, supposing you was alone who'd be in charge then?" (Bang!) and, as Punch might say, "Collapse of stout party who thought he was dancing a polka and found that he had trodden on a banana skin."

(6) The stages of training are roughly (a) elementary drill with or without arms; (b) drilling as a squad; (c) handling arms and loading and firing dummy ammunition. What is generally known as Weapon Training

begins when the recruit has been passed by his Instructor as ready to start his musketry.

"Weapon training" for the H.G. now involves many different types of weapon, but the most important still remains the rifle.

Once the men are fairly proficient with their arms, Collective Training starts in earnest.

Parade ground drill and movements should be kept to a minimum. We are not all asked to mount guard at Buckingham Palace—we only need to be sufficiently well drilled to slope arms, order arms, trail arms, stand at ease and to march in step at the slope.

In the Royal Artillery, to which I had the honour to belong, we considered drill with "hand-guns" of very secondary importance, and when years ago we were suddenly ordered to give up "drill as for Rifle Regiments" in favour of "rifle drill as for Line Regiments," a distinguished gunner officer said it would make very little difference, "because whereas we used to slope past at the trail, we should in future trail past at the slope." That was only a way of upholding the standard of our proper weapons, and there was nothing sloppy about *that*.

(7) Drill must not be left behind on the parade ground. It is still essential everywhere but the more we get down to business the less formal it need be—for example, the mounting of heavy rails in a road-block is a splendid example of drill but there is no barrack square stuff about it.

(8) Training now breaks up into different channels—eventually to converge again in the finished article. Various branches are (a) musketry and weapon training; (b) simple tactics: observation, concealment and report, patrolling and scouting, fieldcraft and occupation of posts, defence, delaying action, attack; (c) maps; (d) simple field fortification; (e) bombs and explosives, anti-tank measures; (f) communication, message forms, telephone, signalling; (g) miscellaneous duties.

When all these have been mastered and our Home Guard is passed fit for service it might be supposed that his training is finished. Not a bit, it is never finished, he can learn something new to-morrow.

(9) We are getting more and more types of machine gun, grenade and bomb, and other delights, but the Home Guard must get really familiar with loading and handling their rifles regularly by day and night; also in using spades, picks, etc., to dig cover.

(10) Fieldcraft. The Home Guard must develop the instincts of the

primitive hunter. If the hunter failed he lost his dinner. If the Home Guard fails he will lose his life. War, in whatever form, is a battle of wits—therefore the Home Guard must be **alert, inquisitive** and **observant**. He must learn the **use of ground**—how to take cover and hide himself both when moving about and when stationary. How to see without being seen. How to remain motionless for long periods. How to use his cunning. How to do without smoking at night. Officers must take the men out in the country and teach them how to do this—pit one man against another first—then one section against another and so on—hide and seek.

Every man can be alert and inquisitive. Some are born to be unobservant, but they can be trained. A good illustration of the unobservant kind is given by the young man who was taking his girl for a drive and the car stopped. So he climbed out and crawled underneath, and as he did not seem to be doing any good she crawled in to help him. Presently a policeman tapped him on the shoulder and said, "Oi! somebody's stolen your car."

You can't expect everybody to notice everything.

(11) Night work. Most of our movement will be at night. Therefore men should be taken out for **short** periods now to get accustomed to moving about in the dark; knowing where they are in the dark; to getting into their road blocks; finding their way to their defence posts. O.P.s, etc., in the dark.

(12) Guides. Every village should have "Guides" who know the country round about and are capable of guiding the reinforcing troops both by day and night. These guides should be well trained in map reading.

(13) Gas. The enemy will probably use gas. Therefore, practise doing ordinary work in gas masks. The civilian gas mask is reasonably good—certainly very much better than nothing.

(14) By this time platoon and section Commanders probably know who are the best men in the detachment. Such men should be earmarked and perhaps specially trained to replace their present Commanders in the event of the latter becoming casualties.

(15) Each of the special aspects of Training is dealt with in great detail further on.

(B) LEADERSHIP.

(1) A good Leader will carry through an action though his men are tired and wet, hungry, thirsty and unwashed, and have been hammered to bits.

(2) Efficiency is a ladder in which every rung must be sound. From the Commander, through the Leaders and the Non-commissioned Ranks to the rank and file, no rung must be allowed to let down the others.

(3) A good Warrant Officer or N.C.O. can pull a bad officer through on parade, but in battle he cannot—like one rotten apple in a barrel, contamination spreads. Cast out the rotten apples. The first duty of a leader is to train himself in his duties by work and study; his second is to train his men on the model he has set himself.

(4) Encourage men to think for themselves, once they know their trade.

"Why did you not do so and so?" "I did not think . . ." "Well, you damned well should think."

"Why did you do so and so?" "Well, sir, I thought." "Well you are not paid to think."

It is apt to be confusing unless we know the true meaning of "Initiative." Initiative is the intelligent exercise of judgment by a man who knows his trade, knows his orders, knows what his superior would do in the altered circumstances of the moment if he were there, and who has the courage to act on his own responsibility.

(5) Encourage the right kind of "swank." Build up *esprit de corps* by self-respect, pride and smartness and a sense of superiority.

Do not be too much of a schoolmaster. Get your young entry to tell *you* things and to swap views. A mother who makes up her mind to have a heart-to-heart talk with her 16-year-old daughter may learn a lot, and so may you.

Let every Commander and man aspire to being the best man in the best Platoon, or in the best Battalion. He must **train and train** or he has not a hope.

(6) **Initiative. Knowledge, technical skill, determination, self-confidence, moral courage and above all—guts**—these are the qualities required in a Commander and in every member of the H.G. The basis of efficiency is organisation, discipline and individual effort—this applies equally to a unit or to one man holding a rifle pit, he must organise his resources, he must exercise that most difficult discipline of all—the

discipline of self; and on his individual effort may depend the security of the whole line.

(C) ORDERS.

(1) **Orders**, whether written or verbal, should be clear, concise and complete.

Clear, means clear to the meanest intelligence.

Concise, means that everything unnecessary is left out.

Complete, means that nothing important is omitted.

If written, get somebody to read them and repeat them in his own words. The more stupid your critic, the better.—Keep a tame B.F. for this purpose.

If verbal (except of course when the orders are to be acted on at once) let the person who is to carry out the order write them down and read them out. If O.K. initial them.

Be precise in specifying times, places and objectives. Never be indefinite. For "dawn" say 07.00 hours, or whatever it is. Say 12.30 or 23.45 hours. Never say "as soon as possible"—say *when*.

Write names of places in block capitals—thus: PULBOROUGH.

(2) Written orders **must be legible**. The recipient may have to read them in the dark. The bearer of a written order should read it out and memorize it in case of accidents.

(3) "Operation Orders" are dealt with in a later chapter. Just as written orders must be "legible," so verbal orders must be "audible." If you want an example of what is wrong in "inaudibility" and "illegibility" go to one of our Courts of Summary Jurisdiction and look and listen. In the H.G. we want to be able to hear every word that is spoken and to read every word that is written; do not be deterred by your experience of peace-time Committee Meetings—insist on orders being **legible** or **audible**.

CHAPTER IV
RIFLES.
(A) The Rifle. (B) Grenade Discharger.
(C) Browning Automatic .300 Rifle.
(D) Firearm Certificates.

(A) THE RIFLE.

(1) The H.G. is armed with one or other of these rifles:

(a) Enfield Pattern 1914 (or P14) .303.

(b) So-called "Springfield."* American-made model of (a) named "Pattern '17"—identical with (a) except for a different model of cartridge and bore .300.

(c) A modern short Lee-Enfield, .303.

(d) Canadian "Ross Rifle" .303.

(a) P14 and (b) Pattern '17 may be considered together because they handle the same and are practically indistinguishable except for the different bore and the different model of cartridge. P14 is not, as commonly supposed, the "Ross Rifle," which will be described below.

They must never be mixed in the same unit owing to the confusion of ammunition.

The Pattern '17 is, for safety, distinguished by a red band painted near the muzzle.

(2) The "Ross" with which the Canadians were armed in 1914, is similar in shape, but it has a "straight-pull" action which tends to jam with mud. It was, therefore, abandoned and, to simplify manufacture in Canada and the States, a rifle (already under tests in this country) was adopted which embodied points common to the Lee-Enfield, the Ross and the American Springfield. This was the P14.

This was never issued to the troops in quantities but only to snipers and (since 1935) to N.R.A.; hence our lack of familiarity with it.

It is more accurate than any previous service rifle: it differs from the short Lee-Enfield in being longer, heavier and less handy and rather tricky to load, but on the other hand its sighting and accuracy are superior. An intelligent man with a fair knowledge of any rifle can learn its tricks in a matter of minutes. The same applies to Pattern '17.

* Footnote: The official American designation is: "United States Rifle Caliber .30, Model of 1917." We call it "Pattern '17," or "P17" for short.

(3) The tricks can be illustrated at once by giving each man in a squad (including the Instructor) these tasks:

(a) Load one round of dummy and fire it.

(b) Load one clip of dummy and fire five aimed shots. Reload one clip.

(c) Load one clip for guard or patrol, so that the magazine contains five rounds, the chamber is empty and the bolt is "home" and not cocked.

A large proportion of trained H.G. will fumble, and once a cartridge jams it is difficult to remove quickly. Picture to yourself a man on patrol, in the dark on a rainy night, who has to load in a hurry and who gets a jam. It is better to be sure than sorry.

(4) These are the tips:—

(a) Any clips and cartridges (dummy or live rounds) for immediate use should be wiped over with an oily rag or rolled in oily fingers—this will reduce jams to a minimum.

(b) To load one round NEVER put it "up the spout." If you hold the muzzle up—as you should—the round will very likely jam. The single round, or indeed any number of loose rounds, **must** be loaded into the magazine with the right thumb in the same way as a clip-full.

(c) To load a clip make sure the clip is in its grooves and press right home into the magazine all five rounds, exerting the thumb pressure *close to the clip* to avoid throwing the cartridges out of line. Close the bolt with a slam and the clip is ejected and the first round loaded. Learn to load smoothly, but move the bolt backwards and forwards with a slam. There are some women who like to be "treated rough"—the P17 is one of these, and all the better for it.

(d) To charge the magazine and leave the rifle safe for guard or patrol, load the clip as described above, then put the fingers (NOT the thumb) of the left hand on top of the uppermost cartridge in the magazine, pressing it down and enabling you to slide the bolt forward, over the top of the uppermost cartridge, as far as it will go. Then, instead of ramming the bolt home and cocking, push the bolt home with the right thumb behind the cocking piece and the right fore-finger pulling the trigger. Close down the knob and the rifle is charged and safe.

(e) Do not shoot your Instructor, he is doing his best. Therefore, always use the right fore-finger to move the safety catch. If you use the thumb the fore-finger strays instinctively to the trigger which is dangerous. Here I come up against experienced Instructors. They say the old drill was to use the thumb, and anyway it does not matter if we do shoot a few Platoon Commanders. I quite agree—but for men not habituated to the use of rifles, I still think my method safest—unless there is somebody you particularly want to shoot. I knew a very experienced Scottish Instructor in "demolitions" once who explained that you must not insert the detonator and fuze like this—but like this—he did it the wrong way round to show how it should not be done. You would have thought that would be the last thing he would do—you would have been right in your surmise—it was the last thing he did do.—Another Scotch mist.

(5) Modern patterns of the short magazine Lee-Enfield (S.M.L.E.) have the same sight as the P14.

(6) The Ross Rifle .303 has a straight pull, *i.e.*, the bolt slides backwards and forwards without the bolt lever being raised; it is, therefore, quicker in action, but has the tendency to jam. Be very careful to keep the bolt clean. The sights are rather similar to P14. The H.G. should use the battle-sight (with leaf down) for all service purposes. It is good up to 600 yards. For target shooting use the aperture, with leaf up, and with the slide adjusted to the range marked on the rear of the leaf. The other refinements of the sight are only for experts under the guidance of instructors.

(7) **The Bayonet** is an additional weapon which H.G. ought to carry, not merely for "bayonet-fighting," but because it is a good tool for breaking open doors, windows, etc., and for getting through obstacles and other purposes. If you have no bayonet carry a bill-hook or hand-axe or a pair of wire-cutters. One of the best utility tools is a "machete," which is a heavy chopper shaped like a hay-knife (with scabbard, 2/6). The old entrenching-tool is not to be despised for all purposes—they were available for 1/6 in 1940, but I hope they have all been bought up by H.G.

(8) **Ammunition.** All these rifles, except Pattern '17, shoot ordinary service .303 cartridges, with a rim. These may be issued in clips or loose; be accustomed to loading clips or single rounds.

Pattern '17 shoots rimless cartridges. If you load the wrong type of cartridge you may get a jam needing an armourer's attention.

(9) **Dummy Ammunition.** This might more properly come under a different heading, but it will do no harm here.

Every man who wants to be an efficient rifle-man should constantly load and fire (at a mark) clips and single rounds of dummy—it is the secret of making the motions of loading and firing automatic. Commanders and Instructors should therefore encourage this in and out of season. There is great pleasure in finding yourself capable of firing off three clips—all of the rounds well aimed—while your neighbour (maybe an old soldier) is still fiddling about with his first clip. Apart from the personal pleasure, which one is more likely to kill enemies?

(10) The man who has only fired five rounds on the range, but who has fired a thousand rounds of dummy is better than the man who has fired fifty rounds and is too lazy or superior to practise with dummy.

A good competition for indoors is to load and fire dummies against time.

(B) GRENADE DISCHARGER.

The Home Guard have now all kinds of weapons, which can be divided into two categories: (*a*) Team weapons, such as the Bombard, Northover projector, M.G., and (*b*) personal weapons such as the rifle, bayonet, B.A.R., tommy gun, pistol, etc.

I am not concerned here with team weapons except to say that for each weapon there should be in each platoon or section to which such a weapon is issued *at least* two (preferably three) teams trained to take over the duties of any gun-number at short notice. In the Home Guard, the reason for this is that you cannot rely on all the members of a particular team turning up on a training parade, you cannot rely on having a full team available in action and you have got to be able to maintain the weapon in action or to keep up continuity of training by having a reserve of men who can take over the duty of casualties and to make up a team.

Each of these individual Home Guard should be, first and foremost, a master of his rifle or other personal weapon and, secondly, capable at a moment's notice of taking over service of his team's weapon.

It is with personal weapons I wish to deal. Our Home Guard is primarily a rifleman who can effectively handle any rifle he is likely to use—S.M.L.E., P 14, P 17, Ross—all are one to him. He may also be trained to use a tommy gun or B.A.R. or pistol and to sling grenades or bombs, but whatever is his particular fancy or whatever he is detailed to do it would be as well for him to understand that he can add to the power of his rifle, which can only fire one bullet at a time, by learning the use of the rifle as a grenade discharger which may stop a vehicle or seriously damage a tank.

The principle is as old as the hills. With a bow our forefathers could shoot an arrow, or an arrow with an incendiary head, or an arrow with a bomb at the end.

With a rifle you can fit to the muzzle a cup which will take grenades of suitable size and weight. A blank cartridge will project that grenade a considerable distance which has a different effect to a bullet and whose trajectory bears no relation to the trajectory of the bullet for which the rifle was designed.

That is the essence of the thing we know as the "discharger." You may use the rifle as a rifle should be used and by fitting the cup you can switch to a different kind of fire action and either drop a Mills grenade amongst personnel far beyond throwing distance or, alternatively, use a H.E. grenade against a vehicle which no bullet would even dent. And you can switch back to rifle fire at short notice.

The first bayonet was a spike which was jammed into the muzzle of a musket which then became a pike incapable of being used as a firearm. Ingenuity then devised a bayonet which fitted round the muzzle instead of inside it and this allowed the musket to be used as a pike *or* as a musket according to circumstances.

The earliest forms of rifle-grenade (long before the last war) consisted of grenade and a long stem which was thrust into the muzzle. A cartridge was loaded into the breech (either with or without the bullet, according to fancy) the discharge certainly projected the grenade, but equally certainly either burst or bulged the barrel.

Then the authorities fitted a cup attachment to the muzzle, and the procedure was to project the grenade by the use of a blank cartridge which did not necessarily bulge the barrel.

And now we have reached the stage—I suppose universal throughout the world—where a proportion of riflemen are equipped with a discharger which can be clipped on to the muzzle so that the rifleman can alternatively fire bullets or grenades.

Our service discharger was designed for the S.M.L.E. and could be clipped on to the nose-cap. The nose-cap is rigid and it does not matter much whether the internal adjusting screw is screwed tight or not so long as the discharger is screwed tight. The rifle and discharger are rigid together. But with the P 14 and P 17 (which have no nose cap) the discharger must be clipped to an adaptor which fits loosely to the muzzle round the foresight. The only way to make the discharger rigid is to screw it tight and also to screw the adjusting screw tight.

Here are my rules for guidance of Home Guards—fortified by experiment:—

Fit the adaptor to the P 14 or P 17 (you will find it waggles).

Clip on the discharger and screw it home, then screw home the adjusting screw. *The discharger is then rigid* and you can fire Mills or any other grenades with a clear conscience.

The rifle to be used with a discharger requires reinforcing to prevent splitting of the stock by the heavy recoil from a ballistite or similar blank cartridge. This is a job for the Ordnance. The stock is bound with wire or straps, just as one straps the handle of a bat or racquet; it is then safe to fire Mills grenades, fitted with a gas check, or the heavier H.E.

The Mills is comparatively light and has a time fuse, i.e., it will burst after 4 or 7 seconds, according to pattern, and will do damage to personnel.

The H.E. grenade is heavier and requires a heavier punch to rupture the shear wire in the fuse so that the fuse can operate on impact.

There is a different technique in each case.

Firing the Mills the rifle is held firmly at an angle of about 45 degrees, the trigger-guard uppermost, and variations of range are obtained by varying the opening of the gas-port of the discharger. The rifle is in fact used as a mortar (or lob-bowler) to drop grenades on personnel.

Firing the heavier H.E. the rifle is actually aimed, with special sights, at the target and the fire is *direct* and not high angle.

In both cases the procedure in the manuals must be followed, but I give this special warning—the butt of the rifle must be firmly bedded against something solid like sandbags, but with H.E. the kick is so formidable that there should be a cushion between butt and sandbags (for example, some sods or a soft partially-filled sandbag) to avoid damage to the stock.

A further warning is that the hands must be clear of metal parts of the rifle to avoid serious cuts due to the powerful kick. The proper hand grip must be learnt from the Instructor, but whatever you do avoid the chance of damage to your hands.

If you have mastered this technique you have got a rifle which can always be used as a rifle or as a grenade thrower, that is, the personal weapon embraces three instruments which employ alternatively—the bullet, the man-killing grenade, and the vehicle stopper.

Now a few words about the cartridge which propels the grenade.

In the old days we used an ordinary blank cartridge or a live round with the bullet removed. Nowadays we use a so-called "ballistite" cartridge.

"Ballistite" is not a general term for powders with a special kick; it is a particular form of propellant which was used in my young days for shooting geese or even game birds that were supposed to require something more powerful or quicker than the normal sporting powders. It consists of square grains with a highly polished black lustre and can thus be easily identified when compared with other sporting or service powders. We need not bother about the chemical composition because we use, quite happily, all kinds of powder—E.C., Smokeless Diamond, Schultze and even propellants such as cordite which are not powders at all.

At one time ballistite was the official favourite for cartridges that required punch, but if you examine a cartridge labelled "ballistite" you will probably find it contains a powder quite indistinguishable from the U.S.A. service powder which is a pyro-cellulose composition.

The fact is that to score a place-kick with a grenade from a discharger it does not matter two hoots what the cartridge is filled with or what it is called so long as it gives the grenade in the discharger the necessary impetus to drop the grenade on the target you want to hit.

Wherefore practise with the cartridges available, and work out for yourselves how you are to make certain of hitting Boches or Boche vehicles with whatever grenades or cartridges are issued to you, and do not bother about what they are called.

(C) BROWNING AUTOMATIC .300 RIFLE.

(1) Chief characteristics are rapidity and accuracy; fired as a single-shot rifle, each shot being fired by pressing the trigger. Since the ejection of empty cartridge and loading are automatic no motion of loading and unloading is necessary as in the rifle with a bolt action.

(2) There is a "change lever" with choice of three positions: at "F" the trigger must be pressed for each round. This is the normal rapid rate. At "A" pressure on the trigger fires a continuous stream of rounds until the pressure is relaxed. At "S" the gun is **safe** and cannot be fired.

(3) For H.G. "A" action, i.e., bursts of fire, will very rarely be used. Accuracy is greatly interfered with and the expenditure of ammunition is prohibitive.

(4) The maximum rate of fire (single rounds) is about 40 well-aimed rounds a minute.

(5) H.G. do not require ever to use any sight except the "battle-sight," and the same remarks already made about the service rifles apply.

(6) Instructional notes have been issued with each rifle and no further details need be given here.

NOTE ON CLEANING OF B.A.R.

The B.A.R. is a reliable weapon in every way, but is apt to give unsatisfactory service if the gas regulator is neglected—however careful the cleaning and oiling of barrel and action.

The gas regulator is like the governor of an engine or the escapement of a watch; any clogging of this part will interfere with the movement.

After firing—even few rounds—the gas regulator must be removed, cleaned and oiled with the greatest care. Whether fired or not it should be examined and cleaned once a week.

Two tools are issued with the B.A.R. of which many H.G. do not know. One is a rimer and cleaner for the gas regulator, which also embodies a peg of the correct diameters to clear the gas ports and holes. The other is a spanner for gas regulator and the flash eliminator.

Other causes of jamming may be (a) the front end of piston sticking in the forward end—remedy, keep the piston clean and oiled.

(b) Cartridge jamming in chamber. The chamber is rather inaccessible for cleaning, and therefore apt to collect rust or debris. The only remedy is to make sure the chamber is cleaned. The best tool is a home-made one consisting of a scourer screwed on to a bit of cleaning rod bent round at approximately a right angle, similar to the brush which is sold for cleaning rifle breeches.

No foresight protector is supplied, and I recommend a short open-ended leather sheath fitting tightly. It costs only a few pence.

It is not generally known that when the rifle is stripped the barrel can be unscrewed and taken out. This, of course, affords a perfect opportunity to ensure that the chamber is cleaned. It should only be done by an armourer. I do not, however, recommend this to be done very often, as I have a prejudice against unscrewing barrels, though this is open to correction by an expert.

This warning must be borne in mind—if you do unscrew the barrel see that it is again screwed *right home*. A mysterious instance of cartridge cases coming asunder in the chamber with resultant jam was traced to the barrel being one turn short of the proper position.

One last word. All American weapons are very greedy for oil. Make sure that they are kept swimming in honest thin oil, like Rangoon—*not* grease or graphite preparations.

(D) FIREARM CERTIFICATES.

Firearm Certificates. H.G. being "part of the armed forces of the Crown" require no firearm certificate and no gun licence for carrying and using any weapon issued to them or approved by their Commander.

The only circumstances in which a firearm certificate is required are when a H.G. wishes to obtain possession of a rifle or revolver from a dealer or a certificated owner. In this case a certificate is required, to be issued or varied. But the following official note on the Firearms Act, 1937, says that such certificate shall be granted without fee.

"A person in the naval, military or air service who satisfies the Chief Officer of Police that he is required to PURCHASE or ACQUIRE a firearm or ammunition FOR HIS OWN USE IN HIS CAPACITY AS SUCH is, by paragraph (b) of Section 5 to be granted a certificate **without fee**. In general an applicant for such a certificate should produce a document issued by his commanding officer showing that he is required to purchase the firearm or ammunition."

It should be noted that in such cases the chief officer* has no discretion to refuse to grant a certificate.

CHAPTER V
(A) Elementary Drill. (B) Platoon Training.
(C) Battle Drill.

(A) ELEMENTARY DRILL.

DRILL FOR RECRUITS TRAINING.

WITHOUT ARMS.

Fall in and stand at ease.
Position of Attention.
Turnings.
Dressing.

Saluting.
Marching.
Marking Time. Halt.
Wheeling.

WITH ARMS.

The Order.
Stand at ease and easy.
The slope. Orders from the slope.
Inspection Port Arms.
Order from the Port.
Long and Short Trail.

Salute when carrying a Rifle.
Ground Arms.
Sling Arms across the body and
on the Shoulder.
Fixing and Unfixing Bayonets.*

When there is sufficient space, Platoons, Squads, etc., will always fall in at intervals ready to march off.

By Captain A. R. S. Hayne, Storrington H.G.

(1) Every recruit must acquire the art of handling his rifle with ease. At first it will be a heavy lump of wood and steel in his hands, but after much patient practice and careful remembrance of instructions it will become almost animate in his hands.

(2) **Order.** Rifle held vertically at the right side, butt on the ground, toe in line and near to the toe of the right foot. Right arm slightly bent, the hand to hold the rifle at, or near, the lower band. **Note:** It is of utmost importance that instructions for the "Order" are strictly carried out to enable other rifle exercises to be performed with ease and simplicity.

---

* This is not going against our official instructions. There is no need for H.G. to go through the old ritual of fixing bayonets, but every recruit must be taught during his elementary training the quickest way of slamming the bayonet on to the rifle. And, be it remembered, no bayonets of any rifle the H.G. is likely to use are interchangeable (except P 17 and P 14) and every H.G. must know how to fix bayonets on any rifle he may have to use.

(3) **Attention.** Heels together and in line. Feet turned out at an angle of 45 degrees. Knees straight. Body erect. Rifle at the order.

(4) **Stand at ease.** Keeping the legs straight, carry the left foot about 12 inches to the left. At the same time incline the muzzle of the rifle to the front with the right arm close to the side.

Troops will always fall in at the "Order," obtain their dressing and then "Stand at ease."

On receiving the order "Attention," the left foot will be brought up to the right and the rifle returned to the Order.

(5) **Slope Arms.** Give the rifle a straight cant upwards from the "Order" with the right hand, catching it with the left hand at the lower band and the right hand at the small of the butt, thumb to the left, elbow to the rear.

Carry the rifle across the body with the right hand, and place it flat on the left shoulder, magazine outwards. At the same time seize the butt with the left hand, the first two joints of the fingers grasping the upper side of the butt, thumb above the toe of the butt, upper part of left arm close to the side, lower part horizontal (upper and lower parts of arm should form a right angle).

Cut away the right hand to the side.

(6) **Order Arms from the Slope.** Drop the rifle to the full extent of the left arm, at same time meeting it with the right hand at the lower band, arm close to the body.

Carry the rifle to the right side, seizing it at the same time with the left hand at the upper band. If the right hand is almost fully extended, it can be taken for certain that the butt will be as near to the ground as required.

Place the butt quietly on the ground, cutting the left hand away to the side.

(7) **Inspection of Arms.** "For-Inspection-Port-Arms" Cant the rifle, muzzle leading, with the right hand, smartly across the body, guard to the left and downwards, the barrel crossing opposite the left shoulder, and meet it at the same time with the left hand close to the point of balance, thumb and fingers round the rifle, both elbows close to the body. Push up the safety catch with the forefinger, knock up the knob of the bolt and withdraw it to the full extent. Then grasp the butt with the right hand immediately behind the bolt, thumb towards the muzzle.

(8) **Ease-Springs.** Lower the left hand to the magazine, depress the magazine with the first 3 fingers, pass the bolt over and thrust home until it reaches the cocking position. **Ease the trigger spring by pressing the**

trigger, at the same time pushing the bolt home by the thumb on the cocking piece. Bring the safety catch back with the forefinger. Carry the left hand back to the point of balance.

(9) **Order Arms from the Port.** Holding the rifle firmly in the left hand, seize it with the right at the lower band.

Carry the rifle to the right side with the right hand as in the second motion of the Order from the Slope.

(10) **Trail Arms from the Order.** By a slight bend of the right arm give the rifle a cant forward and seize it at the point of balance, bringing it at once to a horizontal position at the side at the full extent of the right arm, which should hang easily, fingers and thumb round the rifle.

(11) **Order Arms from the Trail.** Raise the muzzle, slip the right hand up to the lower band and come to the Order.

Note: The Trail is only used (Rifle Regiments excepted) for movements in the field in close and extended order.

(12) **Change Arms from the Trail.** Bring the Rifle to a vertical position in front of the right shoulder, magazine to the front, upper part of the arm close to the side, forearm horizontal.

Throw the rifle across the front of the body to the left side, catching it with the left hand at the point of balance, at same time cutting the right hand smartly to the side. In this position the rifle is held perpendicularly opposite the left shoulder, magazine to the front, upper part of the left arm close to the side, left forearm horizontal.

Lower the rifle to the full extent of the left arm at the trail.

(13) **Right Turn.** Turn to the right by swivelling on the right heel and left toe, raising the heel and toe in doing so, the weight of the body on the right foot.

Bring the left heel smartly up to the right without stamping the foot on the ground.

(14) **Left Turn.** Turn to the left by swivelling on the left heel and right toe, carrying on as for Right Turn.

Bring the right heel smartly to the left.

(15) **About Turn.** Turn to the right-about on the right heel and left toe, raising the left heel and right toe in doing so.

On completion of this preliminary movement, the right foot must be flat on the ground and the left heel raised.

Bring the left heel smartly up to the right.

(16) **Incline to the Right or Left.** Make a half turn to right or left.

(17) **Right Turn on the March.** Turn to the right on the left foot and to the left on the right foot.

(18) **About Turn on the March.** Turn right about on your own ground, in 3 beats of time, and move forward a full pace on the fourth beat.

(19) **March Discipline.** Troops will always march off the parade ground at the Slope. As soon as this has been done the order "March at Ease" should be given. When marching at ease the rifle may be carried in any way the soldier fancies. Never tire men by marching at the slope.

(20) **In the Field. Large parties** will move in Extended Order, the Order being "to the **right** or **left**, or from the centre to right and left— paces extend." Each man, except the **right** or **left** or **centre** man, will move off in the given direction. The first man from the pivot man, on completing the number of paces, will touch the shoulder of the man in front of him who will start his pace count and so on to the last man.

(21) **Small parties** will move in single file until the order to extend is given.

(22) **In extended order** rifles must be carried at the trail. Small parties will also carry their rifles at the trail when proceeding in single file.

(23) **All troops** must march in same formation, whether extended order, single file, or two deep, never straggle along like a flock of sheep. In a formation, troops are mobile and ready to take up any position in any direction at a moment.

(24) **At Night** silence is essential.*

(25) All the above may be modified by the new technique of "Battle Drill"—in this book I hope to revise in 1943 the details of drill.

---

* Foot note: This applies to men in movement or on guard or at rest. A noisy sentry may give away the whole show.

Many stories are told about Sentries challenging in the wrong way, *e.g.* "Advance one and sign the counterfoil."

William Hickey, in the *Daily Express* of September 10th, 1940, gives us:—

"Halt! who goes there?"

"Army Chaplain."

"Advance Charlie Chaplin, to be recognised, and don't be so bloody funny next time."

I will not lay down the law about challenging, but I do say: "Do not be audible from Ashington to Chanctonbury Ring," and "realise that you only challenge in order to identify the visitor."

(B) PLATOON TRAINING.
By Lt.-Col. F. J. Wyeth, M.C.

(Here are the views of a man who successfully trained and organised a Platoon before being appointed to command his Battalion. They should be read as sound advice and not as hard and fast instructions as to how to organise or run a Platoon in other circumstances.)

In most of the following paragraphs **principles** only are considered. **Details** are given in respect of only (a) certain formations and movements which are constantly required, and (b) certain cases in which important changes have recently been introduced.

The Platoon, the most important and convenient training unit. In rural areas (a) its personnel normally drawn from single village or district. Local topography well known to men. (b) Few opportunities for training larger units.

ORGANISATION.

The platoon consists of Platoon Commander, 2nd in Command (2nd-Lieut. or Platoon-Sergt.), 3 Section Commanders (Sergts.), and 3 sections.

In a regular infantry battalion the section consists of 7-10 men, *i.e.*, platoon strength of 21-30 men. The H.G. platoon may be much stronger, in which case each section may be divided into 2 or more sub-sections (or squads), each commanded by a corporal or lance-corporal.

When the platoon "falls in" on parade each section forms ONE RANK. The Section Commander is the right file of his section, and if the section be sub-divided each sub-section commander is the right file of his sub-section.

Unit Commanders. Note:—

Efficiency of unit depends upon efficiency of its commander.

Men must (a) be well trained, (b) be well led, (c) have confidence in their commander.

Comfort and welfare of men a primary consideration.

Good discipline without rigidity.

Subordinates encouraged to accept responsibility, and to develop initiative.

Orders clear, brief, decisive.

Tactics rapidly adapted to changes of situation.

When instructing:—	Stand **still** in front of centre of class.
	Speak clearly and slowly.
	Use simple language.
	Avoid repetition of mere text book phrases.
	Show, as well as explain.
	Question men frequently.
	Keep lesson short, with variety of subject.
All ranks. Note:—	Attention to care of arms and equipment.
	Regular attendance, punctuality, keenness.
	Prompt, cheerful obedience. Do not "grouse."
	Commander ready to hear legitimate grievance, but "Obey first: complain afterwards."
	No matter how much you know, be always ready to learn.
	If you do not understand, ask for explanation.

TRAINING.

(a) **Training of N.C.O.'s.** By lectures, and by parades, using selected squad of ex-infantrymen. Facilitates training. Acts as "refresher" for men of squad, who become useful "stiffening" of platoon when it parades as a unit. Constantly refer to preceding paragraph *re* Unit Commanders.

(b) **Training of Recruits.** By N.C.O.'s. Supervision by Pltn. Cr. ensures uniformity: enables him to assess ability of N.C.O.'s. Small squads of various degrees of proficiency. Transfer recruits upwards (or downwards) as desirable.

(c) **Section Training.** Some section training should precede that of Platoon. Section normally trained by Sn. Cdr.

SQUAD DRILL.

General

1. *Three ranks.* Squad drill will be carried out in three ranks unless numbers are insufficient, when two ranks will be formed.

2. *Distance and interval.* Distance between ranks will be 30in.; intervals between men will be obtained by dressing with intervals. (*See below.*)

3. *Dressing.* Normally, dressing will be taken up by each man on completion of a movement without word of command. Only in ceremonial will men wait for the command "Right Dress," "Eyes front."

4. *Taking open and close order.* On the command "Open—order—March," the front rank will take two paces forward, and the rear rank two paces back. On the command "Close—order—March," the action of the front and rear ranks is reversed.

5. *Guides and blank files.* When squads, etc., are turned about, guides and blank files will take three paces forward at the halt, or mark time three paces if on the move. During squad drill in open order, blank files and guides will not alter their positions unless ranks are changed.

6. *Training.* On training, when the order "Quick March" is given, the soldier will come to attention and move off at the sling (right shoulder).

Dressing a squad with intervals

Right—Dress

Each man, except the right-hand man, will turn his head and eyes to the right and at the same time extend his right arm, back of the hand upwards, hand clenched, with the knuckles touching the shoulder of the man on the right (or left). When dressing with the rifle at the order, the left arm will be extended. He will then take up his dressing in line by moving, with short quick steps, till he is just able to distinguish the lower part of the face of the second man beyond him. Care must be taken to carry the body backward or forward with the feet, the shoulders being kept perfectly square in their original position.

Eyes—Front

The head and eyes will be turned smartly to the front, the arm cut away to the side, and the position of attention resumed.

Dismissing

Squad—Dis-miss

The squad will turn to the right and, after a pause equal to four paces in quick time, break off quietly and leave the parade ground in quick time.

If arms are carried, they will be sloped before the dismiss, except on wet days, when men may be dismissed at the order.

Marching in file

Turning into file

Move to the Right (*or* Left) in file. Right (*or* Left)—Turn

The whole will turn to the right (*or* left) and lead on in that direction without checking the pace. The men of the rear rank will dress by their front rank men.

Changing direction by wheeling

Squads or platoons in line should change direction by wheeling.

Changing direction
Change direction Right (*or* Left). Right (*or* Left)—Wheel

The inner man of the leading file will move round a quarter of the circumference of a circle having a radius of four feet, stepping short to enable the outer man of the file to wheel with him. When the quarter circle is completed, the file leads on in the new direction. The other files in succession will follow in the footsteps of the leading file without increasing or diminishing their distances from each other or altering the time.

If the squad is halted, or ordered to mark time, when only a part of it has wheeled into the new direction, the remainder will cover off.

EXTENDED ORDER.

All movements with **"slung"** rifles. Less fatiguing than "trail."

For purpose of preliminary instruction it may be convenient to practise in single rank (arm length extension).

First practise with whistle and verbal commands. Then by whistle and hand signals.

Signals in extended order practice. (See Infantry Section Leading, 1938, pp. 28-31).

(i) **Hand signals:** Advance. Halt. Retire. Incline. Change direction. Double. Quick time. Lie down. Rise. Extend. Close.

(ii) **Whistle signals:** Attention (preparatory to an order). Rally. Alarm.

(iii) **Rifle signals:** No enemy in sight. Few enemy in sight. Many enemy in sight.

RIFLE EXERCISES.

To give variety introduce short periods of rifle exercises among the drill movements described above.

Note *re* **Fixing and Unfixing Bayonets.**

In the first movement of fixing bayonets the *L* arm is **straightened** by partly withdrawing bayonet from scabbard.

In fixing the bayonet the head and eyes are turned to *R* to see that bayonet is fixed. They remain so until the order "Attention" is given.

In unfixing. When returning bayonet to scabbard, turn head and eyes to *L*. They remain so until order "Attention" is given.

JUDGING DISTANCE, VISUAL TRAINING, FIRE CONTROL should be added.

Note.—In carrying out a change of position there is sometimes a possible choice of method. Try to choose the simplest and quickest.

PLATOON DRILL.

(See Figs. 1 and 2.)

1. *A Platoon in line forming column of route*

"Move to the right (*or* left) in column of route"

"Right (*or* Left) Turn—Quick March"

The platoon commander and the platoon serjeant (or 2nd I/C) will move to their positions on the command "Right turn."

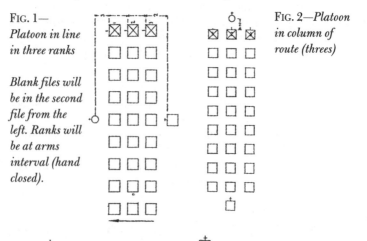

Fig. 1— *Platoon in line in three ranks*

Blank files will be in the second file from the left. Ranks will be at arms interval (hand closed).

Fig. 2—*Platoon in column of route (threes)*

KEY.— ○̇ *Platoon Commander* □ *2nd i/c or Platoon Serjeant.*

2. *A platoon in column of route forming line*

"Platoon will advance—Left turn"

The men act as in squad drill, the platoon commander and platoon sergeant regaining their positions in line in Quick Time.

3. *Other Movements.*—For drill purposes. Platoons will be exercised in the movement detailed for squad drill, the word "Platoon" being substituted for "Squad."

COMPANY DRILL.

1. *A close column when halted forming column of route*

i. **"Advance (or retire) in column of route from the right (*or* left)—Right (*or* left) turn"**

The commander of the leading (*or* rear) platoon will give "*No. . . . Platoon left* (or *right*) *wheel. Quick—March,*" and each platoon commander will act similarly in time to gain his place in column of route.

ii. **"Move to the right (*or* left) in column of route—Right (*or* left) turn"**

The commander of the leading (*or* rear) platoon will give "*No. . . . Platoon. Quick—March,*" and each remaining platoon commander will give "*No. . . . Platoon, left* (or *right*) *wheel. Quick—March*" in time to gain his place in column of threes.

   (*a*) Unless otherwise ordered, a company will move off from the right of the leading platoon, or from the left of the rear platoon.

   (*b*) A company can be marched off from any platoon as follows: "*Advance* (or *retire*) *in column of route in the following order—No. 2, No. 3, No. 1 platoons.*"

2. *A close column when halted moving to a flank in threes.*

"Move to the right (*or* left) in threes. Right (*or* left) turn—Quick—March"

The platoon on the right (*or* left) will direct unless any other platoon is detailed to do so.

3. *A column of route forming close column of platoons at the halt facing a flank.*

"At the halt, facing left, form close column of platoons"

The commander of the leading platoon will halt his unit and turn it to the left by giving "*No. . . . Platoon. Halt. Left turn.*" The remainder will be led by their guides by the shortest route to their positions in close column, where they will receive the command, "*No. . . . Platoon. Halt. Left turn.*" On the word "Halt," the right guides will at once turn to their left and take up their covering and distance from the right guide of the platoon in front.

4. *A company in close column advancing (or retiring) in column.*
i. **"Advance in column"**

The commander of the leading platoon will give "*No. . . . Platoon will advance. By the right. Quick—March,*" and the remaining platoons will be similarly marched off when the platoon next in front has reached column distance.

ii. **"Retire in column." "The company will retire. About—turn"**

Platoon commanders will march their platoons in succession at column distance, giving the command "*No. . . . Platoon. By the left. Quick—March.*"

(B) OPEN OR EXTENDED ORDER.

Moving along a road.

Make use of all cover. Often desirable to move with sections in single file, each section along one hedge (or side of road). Have scouts and connecting files.

Practise rapidly taking cover from air observation.

Advancing across open country. (See Infantry Section Leading, 1938, pp. 39-44).

    (i)   Open column of sections with considerable extension and interval.

    (ii) Sections in single file with considerable interval. Latter preferable when possible to advance along hedgerow or ditch.

    (iii) "Arrowhead" formation.

Extended order.

Movements as in Section training. (See I.S.L., 1938, pp. 33-34).

L.D.V. Training Instructions Nos. 1-6 and 9.

Platoon commanders should constantly refer to these.

Messages and reports. Of utmost importance.

Frequently practise men (and especially N.C.O.'s).

Clarity, brevity, completeness essential.

Carefully study **Home Guard Message Form**.

Guard commander should always write up a Guard Report.

Guard mounting to be practised.

Movement and taking up defensive positions by night must be frequently practised. (See I.S.L., 1938, pp. 34-37).

Men advancing in line should sling rifles and hold hands.

Advancing in file—hold a long length of string.*

Following also important:—

Duties of Outposts, Protective Detachments (formerly Pickets), **Observation Posts, Patrols, Sentries.** (See Infantry Section Leading, 1938, pp. 47-54).

A platoon is a convenient unit for practising a complete **Outpost.**

From front to rear:—

(i)   Sentries } one sub-section.
(ii) Observation post

(iii) Protective detachment—2 sub-sections.

(iv) Reserve—remainder of platoon.
         (This provides **Patrols**).

(v)   MAIN BODY.

> Distances may be:—Between (i) and (ii) 20-30 yds., between (ii) and (iii) 200-300 yds., between (iii) and (iv) 400 yds., (iv) and (v) depends on nature of locality and tactical situation, 800-1,000 yds.

It is essential in every case that commander should first carefully describe and explain his dispositions and intentions.

Men must be tested by questions and encouraged to ask for further explanations if required.

Practice in "shadowing" an Advancing (or Retiring) Enemy, and in sending information to Unit Commander.

(N.B.—Impress on men the necessity for "keeping to a flank" of the enemy.)

---

* Or hold the end of the bayonet scabbard of the man in front. (Obstacles or rough ground may prevent these precautions).

(C) BATTLE DRILL.

"Battle Drill" under that name is new to the Home Guard though much of it is familiar in principle under the old description, "Fire and Movement." Old soldiers will also remember the formations used in the last war, such as arrowhead formation and artillery formation.

In some form or other it is as old as war itself and if we had access to the records of the Light Brigade in the Peninsular War we should find much that is supposed to be new.

It would be inadvisable to publish here a complete Battle Drill for H.G. for two reasons—(1) all available papers vary and none of them legislate particularly for H.G. organization and weapons, (2) it is understood that an official manual is shortly to be produced for Home Guard use and it would be unwise to anticipate it by anything unauthoritative which would only lead to confusion.

I have, however, inserted some notes by an officer who had had very recent experience of the most up-to-date Army School teaching.

NOTES ON BATTLE DRILL.
by
Captain S. M. Pemberton, Adjutant, 4 Sussex H.G.

Battle Drill is a new approach to training. It seeks to bring the training 'on the square' into line with actual battle movements. It is a deliberately stereotyped Drill based on the patterns of modern war.

It must always be remembered that it is a *DRILL*, and its value for the inculcation of discipline will only be preserved if the utmost attention is paid to smartness of all movements.

It aims at imbuing troops with the "Team Spirit," at the same time teaches that each man has an individual job to do, but all with the same object, that of isolating and disposing of the enemy.

"One leg on the ground" is a slogan worth remembering—and if carried out every man will be assured that each time he moves, his pal is keeping the enemy's heads down or diverting their attention to the best of his ability and affording him a measure of protection, so that his movement may be carried out with greater *SPEED*, which is essential in modern warfare. Hence the reason that once the actual movements and positions have been mastered, the drill should, in normal circumstances, be executed at the double. Instructors should check slovenly action or handling of weapons.

The Drills usually practised are for:—

Squad or Section—Flanking, Left or Right. House Clearing.

Platoon—Pincer, Tank Laager Attack. Wood Searching. Street Clearing.

These may be carried further to Company training, but Home Guards, generally, will find that it is better to stick to the smaller units.

The simplest form of teaching should be used so as to enable a lot of ground to be got over in the short hours available for training Home Guards.

If the following rules are used it will be found that a great deal of efficiency will be obtained in a surprisingly short time.

Each Squad or Section should consist of a Commander (Sergeant or Corporal) and 10 other ranks divided into two Groups, Assault and Fire, the former consisting of the Commander, Riflemen and Bombers, the latter the Second in Command, B.A.R. and Sniper.

The Second in Command may also be an N.C.O. Each man in the initial stages should be labelled in a similar way to which a football team is numbered, but in this case with such titles at No. 1 Rifleman, No. 2 B.A.R., Sniper, etc., and when numbering should step forward one pace and shout his designation, thus:—

> No. 2 Rifleman, Assault Group.
>
> No. 1 B.A.R., Fire Group.

Then the training ground should be marked out in the form of a square 100 yds. x 100 yds. and marked at the appropriate points with lettered boards thus:—

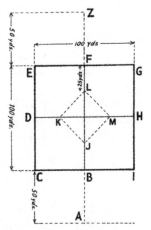

The forming up line is at A and the enemy at Z, who should be represented by L rifleman lying, preferably with a few rounds of blank, for flanking or pincer movements, and by riflemen singly and in pairs for Wood Searching, with the addition of boxes to represent tanks when practising an attack on a Tank Laager.

House and Street Clearing Drills cannot be carried out other than in actual buildings, but suitable places are not, as a rule, difficult to find in most districts.

Words of command should be as brief as possible and given in the early stages by the Instructor, though normally the Squad or Platoon Commander, and always followed by "Any Questions," before the final word to move.

An instance in the case of a Flanking movement. Squad, having formed up astride "A" and numbered "for Battle Drill," "Right Turn—Left Wheel—Quick March—Enemy—Open Fire."

When first man reaches line C—B—I, his Squad form line facing Z at Ease. The whole shout "Down—Crawl—Observe."

Instructor then gives order, "Enemy—50 yds. N.—We will attack. Right flanking. Fire Groups here. Any Questions?—Follow me."

After having executed the prescribed movements, the final word of command is "Reorganisation," when the Squad reforms on the Commander, who leads them back to base at "A." Hardly more than a dozen orders are given throughout this Drill yet every man should be perfectly clear as to his function, and his interest will have been maintained throughout.

It may be found that added interest can be given if the Squad is not formed up in the same order for each parade and the men changed about and become a Rifleman one day and a Bomber the next, so that the monotony is broken.

This, however, may not be desirable for the Fire Group where Home Guards are armed with the B.A.R., which is essentially a single shot repeating rifle and not a L.M.G., and should be in the hands of the best shots available.

CHAPTER VI
MUSKETRY.

(A) By Capt. A. R. S. Hayne, Storrington H.G.

(1) **Fire Direction.**

Anticipatory Order. Range—Object—Number of rounds.

Final Order. Clock position from object. Example, object, left, 9 o'clock, two fingers, tree, aim at base.

(2) **Training of Eye.**

(a) **By Day.** This does not require a rifle or a range. All that is needed is a willing spirit. Note and describe objects fairly close at hand: groups of people, colours and shapes of roofs, herds of animals counted. The brain must be trained to take note of what the eyes see. You will be making yourself a better soldier if you see and remember such things as Post Office, Telegraph and Telephone posts, in fact anything that may be of use to an army, defending, attacking or on the march. Use the shortest word to describe an object.

(b) **By Night.** Learn to judge the distance covered by 10, 20, 25, 50 paces. Ability to see in the dark increases by practice.

Objects are more visible when the moon is behind the observer.

An observer may stand up when he has a definite background, and lie down when he has not.

Educate your eyes. Constant practice gives best results.

(3) **Distance Judging.** The judging of distances with fair accuracy is of the utmost importance in warfare.

AVOID guessing. Have a well defined reason for every estimate.

Create standards. Such as, at 80 yds, a man's eyes are visible; at 400 yds. a face is only a dot.

Have a number of standards ready in your mind to meet circumstances. Let the eye become acquainted with 100 yds., then double and treble that distance.

Errors in under-estimation likely:—(a) on bright days, (b) sun behind observer, (c) when looking up or down.

Errors in over-estimation likely:—(a) when observer is kneeling or prone, (b) on misty or dull days, (c) object in the shade, (d) when looking up streets or avenues of trees.

(4) **Rifle Fire.** NEVER rest your rifle on any inanimate object. It makes

the rifle jump after the shot has been fired. Use your rifle sling if you can and rest your left forearm or wrist wherever possible.

When two or more men engage a party of enemy they should take up positions which will give cross fire, never frontal fire.

(5) **Aiming.** Imagine the face of a clock round each object aimed at. Look through the aperture that forms the backsight, place the tip of the blade of the foresight at 6 o'clock of your object. Example: make a clock of a man's face, 6 o'clock would be his chin—the mark on which you place the tip of your foresight.

Some say "Close the disengaged eye," but very many shoot with both eyes open. The latter is less tiring and gives you a chance of seeing what is going on. It is a matter for your own discretion.

(6) **Aiming Rules.** Always take the same amount of foresight into your aperture. The easiest manner in which to do this is to draw an imaginary line through the backsight aperture horizontally and vertically. Bring the tip of your foresight to bear on the point of intersection.

Too much foresight will cause you to shoot high and too little the reverse.

If your rifle is not lying straight in your left palm but canted (slanted) to right or left, your shot will take one or other direction. **Keep your rifle straight.**

See that your rifle is well balanced in your left palm. To obtain this, place the rifle on your palm running diagonally across it. Under the point of balance of the rifle will be found a "shoulder;" this shoulder should fit into the lower right of the palm so that the rifle rests diagonally across the palm. Open the fingers out straight—your rifle should rest perfectly steady in that position, then close your fingers over your rifle and you are ready to take your aim. If the rifle is placed in another position in the palm a perfect balance will not be obtained, nor a sure grip.

See that the butt of your rifle is pressed hard into and well cupped in your shoulder.

Take the **first pull** on the trigger **before** you attempt to align your sight.

Do not hold your breath until you are ready to give the **final** squeeze to your trigger.

(7) **Position.** It is essential to have a comfortable position or stance. Centuries of experience have taught the military authorities the best positions, and these alone must be adopted.

(a) **Standing.** For firing from behind high cover or breastwork. When firing from this position always use your sling. To take up the standing position, turn half right (it must be a correct half right and **not** almost a full right) carry the left foot off to the left slightly forward about 12 ins. (Men over medium height may increase the distance to such as will give their body an even balance). The rifle should next be brought to the right side in front of the hip, with the muzzle pointing upwards. Grasp the small of the butt with the right hand. The stock is grasped by the left hand at the point of balance immediately in front of the magazine.

On the command "Load," push the safety catch forward with the forefinger, never the thumb, and open the breech by withdrawing the bolt. Press the clip into the magazine with the centre of the thumb (not the soft fleshy part of the thumb), which must be at right angles to the cartridges. Make a clean, straight, unhesitating thrust downwards, close to the clip, and there will be no jamming. To aim and fire, the butt of the rifle should be brought into the hollow of the right shoulder and pressed hard home, the right elbow fully extended in line with the shoulder. It must never be dropped, since only when in alignment with the shoulder can a cup be formed by the shoulder and the shoulder-blade for the butt to sit in, and thus obviate any possible slipping when the kick comes after shot has been fired. The left elbow must be brought as near the trigger guard as possible, the forearm forming nearly a right angle with the rifle. The trigger must not be touched till the rifle is squarely in the shoulder.

Standing Position (WRONG).

Criticisms: Body leaning back and cannot take shock of recoil—butt of rifle above shoulder and wound slip. Tip of finger only on trigger. Legs— no balance. Left arm not under rifle and left hand placed on rifle—no grip. No support for rifle.

Try this position and see how long you can hold a rifle up.

Points to remember. (1) A firm, even balance of the body on the feet. (2) Head well back to get the eye as far as possible from the backsight. (3) Firm grip with both hands. These points are the same for every position.

Standing Position (CORRECT).

(1)   Body balanced equally on both feet.

(2)   Butt of rifle in hollow of shoulder. Finger **round** trigger. Right elbow **up**.

(3)   Left arm **under** rifle for support. Hand grasping rifle at point **balance**.

(4)   Butt against right cheek.

(b) **Kneeling.** The Regulations regarding this are as follows: "Kneel on either or both knees. In the former case, the body may be supported on the heel or not as desired; the left knee will be in advance of the left heel, and the left elbow rest on or over the left knee; the left leg, hand and arm, and the right shoulder, should be in the same vertical plane, when firing in the open, kneeling on the right knee. In the latter, the body may rest on both heels, or be kept upright to suit the height of the cover, the elbows in both instances being unsupported by the body." To obtain greater steadiness it is advised that the firer get down on his heel or heels.

(c) **Prone.** Used on open ground and from behind low cover. This position must be taken up with the greatest possible rapidity and without fuss.

(8) **Movement.** Turn half right and bring the rifle across the body with the butt in front of the right hip, as in the standing position. Drop on to both knees, place the right hand on the ground holding the rifle in the left hand. Shoot the legs out to the left rear, so that the stomach comes flat to the ground. The left shoulder must be well forward and both elbows drawn in towards the body, not spread-eagled out. The position of the hands is the same as for standing. To load, drop the **butt** to the ground and lower the left hand a little. On no account must the **muzzle** be lowered to the ground and thus run the risk of getting grit into the muzzle. Loading must be proceeded with as explained in the standing position. To unload, proceed as for loading, keeping a firm grip on the rifle with the left hand. Knock the bolt up and thus avoid jerking the rifle from side to side. The "knock up" increases speed in rapid fire.

(9) **Fire Discipline.** A high standard in the men is not less important than skilful direction and control by Commanders.

Fire discipline means strict attention to the signals and orders of the Commander, combined with intelligent observation of the enemy. It requires deliberate aim, economy of ammunition and prompt cessation of fire when ordered or when the target disappears.

It requires of the men endurance of the enemy's fire, even when no reply is possible; a cool and intelligent use of the rifle when superior control can no longer be exercised (Inf. Training 1914).

(10) **Rapid Fire** should be considered as a reserve of power to be used when the occasion demands it. It must combine accuracy with rapidity.

*   *   *

(B) Some Notes by an old Rifleman of great experience:—Major F. Dickerson, 4 Sussex H.G.

Much H.G. musketry training consists of firing a few rounds at a 4 ft. target. This is not enough to kill boches.

Let us start from where the recruit goes on the open Range for the first time.

He should fire a grouping practice first, to find any fault of the firer or rifle. This should be fired at 100 yds., 5 rounds at the same point of aim. No signalling of shots. The recruit should go and examine his target—if the 5 shots are in a 4-in. or 8-in. ring he has benefitted by his previous instruction and is fit to carry on with application. If they are not, he should be given more instruction. If the centre of the group is more than 12 inches from the point of aim, the rifle should be tested by a skilled shot.

Now the recruit will go to 200 yds. Application. Applying his aim to hit the mark. This is where a good coach is invaluable. He will not pull the recruit into position, worry him with a lot of instruction, help him load his rifle, etc., but will keep away to the right rear of the firer, and watch him fire two rounds before giving advice. He will have a sketch of the target and explain to the firer quietly where the hits are, etc., and let the firer think it out, that if a hit is a foot high right, his next aim will be a foot low left from the point of aim. I have heard instructors say, "Go a bit left and low," the recruit, afraid of going too far, aims perhaps 2 inches left and low and is disappointed, and another, perhaps two, of his precious rounds are fired before he gets the bull. This is the time to make a recruit interested and realize the power of his rifle and value it. After the recruit has proved his ability at application, all his future training should be to learn to be quick and able to hit a small moving target. Explain to him that if the target had moved just as he fired, he would not have hit the bull and the boches won't stand still and his head (big as it is) is not larger than the bull at 200 yds., so he must learn to hit a moving target. A disc on a 6-ft. pole carried along the butts with the disc above the parapet is a good test. Then explain the importance of Rapid Fire. A man's best rate with accuracy depends entirely upon the amount of practice.

The H.G. will not, as a rule, fire over 300 yds., more often less, which means our fire must be quick and accurate or we shall be overrun. The average H.G. can double his rate of accurate fire by practice, which means more than doubling his value as a fighter.

Here are a few tips to increase your rate. Clean the chamber of your rifle to insure easy ejection of the empty case. Draw back the bolt to full extent to allow the round to rise from the magazine. Eye well back from the cocking piece to enable you to open the bolt when in the aim position. After placing the charger in the guides place the thumb on the top cartridge with the four fingers under the rifle and give a steady even pressure between fingers and thumb, this will prevent a jam.

Practise rapid loading without firing on the range with ball ammunition.

Remember, when firing at night, in fog or smoke, aim low.

With the bayonet fixed (which it should be at all distances up to 300)—

With the P 17 rifle, aim *up* 3 inches at 200 yds. With the S.M.L.E. rifle, aim *down* 10 inches at 200 yds.

Positions. After learning to fire in the open, learn to fire from awkward positions, making use of any available cover. Learn to adopt quickly any firing position. How often will a man on service fire his rifle in a position taught on the Range?

Don't waste time adjusting sights—we have a Battle Sight—nor bother about allowing for wind. It will take a gale to put you off your target at 200.

Make good use of your time by learning to aim off for movement.

The H.G.'s first duty is to kill, his second not to be killed, by skilful use of cover from view and fire. I put "view" first for it is the most important. *Don't* give the enemy a target.

(C) RIFLE AND RANGE DISCIPLINE.

The H.G. are now (July, 1941) receiving a continuous flow of new weapons and appliances, and it is a question for serious consideration whether they can learn all these new things efficiently in addition to their older armament, or whether saturation point has not been reached.

The bulk of H.G. are "part-time only," and it is unreasonable to expect them to become as proficient as professional whole-time soldiers. On the other hand, there are some H.G. who put in full time, many of them ex-service men, of whom some are capable of lapping up the new weapons as fast as they come along.

The point is that the majority of H.G. *cannot be expected to learn any more*, in fact will unlearn what they know if an attempt is made to cram them, but there are a certain proportion with sufficient all-round proficiency to become specialists with a larger repertoire. It would therefore appear desirable to limit the issue of new appliances to a scale that the H.G. may be expected to absorb.

That is a matter for the authorities, but here is one for the H.G.—whatever weapons we have got or are getting, the fact remains that our primary, principal and only essential weapon is the rifle (and bayonet), and the first duty of every H.G. is to become master of the rifle with which he is armed—in fact, a professional rifleman.

The time has come to pull ourselves up with a jerk and put this right. It is quite easy if we insist on certain simple rules for what might be called comprehensively "Rifle and Range Discipline."

It is a fact that the rawest recruit, after being passed out from drill, handling arms and .22, can be taught all he need know about the rifle before being put on the open range in two or three *individual* lessons of ¼-hour each on different days.

Our object, then, is to make every H.G. proficient with the rifle with which he is armed, and he must also be taught the peculiarities of the other rifles which may be issued to him or which he may have to use in action owing to, *e.g.*, shortage of .30 ammunition. There are only four such rifles, all fully described on p. 33, and though they differ there is nothing so different as to make it difficult to learn them all.

I maintain that the rifle is the H.G.'s first weapon, and that an instructor has no business to teach him any other weapon till he knows the rifle.

The following are simple rules:—

(1) Every H.G. before firing on the range must be passed out by his Platoon Commander in (*a*) elementary training; (*b*) .22 shooting; and (*c*) dummy loading and firing.

(2) On the range all men waiting their turn to fire should be seen loading and firing at least two clips of dummy in the lying position. (N.B.—Some men who can load standing are all at sea lying.) This can be dispensed with in the case of really proficient men, but it is no hardship to give up a few minutes of a very long "sit-easy" for what is excellent practice. This is an opportunity for small competitions or sweeps. This appears to conflict with the principle that dummy and live ammunition should never be together on the range—but it is quite easy to keep the dummy well away from the firing point.

(3) Rifles must be inspected before proceeding to the firing point and before leaving it. At the firing point, except when loaded and ready to fire, the rifle bolt must always be open.

(4) A responsible skilled officer or N.C.O. must always be on duty at the firing point to see that men adopt the correct position and carry out all the details of loading, firing, sight adjustment, etc., properly, instead of letting the men slop about anyhow. It is a good thing to have a trained coach lying down with each man firing.

CHAPTER VII
NOTES ON ARTILLERY FOR HOME GUARD.

(A) Ordnance. (B) Indirect Fire.

This chapter is strictly unconventional. I offer a few general remarks on Artillery subjects, so that the H.G. can pick out for himself points which may make his work on Spigot Mortar, Mortar, Special Guns and Projectors easier or more interesting. Above all some knowledge of Artillery methods may suggest simpler or more effective handling of team weapons.

(A) ORDNANCE.

From the beginning of time personal weapons have progressed through various stages. The club, the axe, the kelt (the prototype of a broken bottle or a kosh), the hand missile, the missile propelled by mechanical means—sling, catapult, bow or gun—the knife, dagger, sword, spear, rapier, pair of swords—all of these have gone through their apprenticeship and development, and many types having reached their highest point have declined and disappeared, only to re-emerge in some new way of fighting.

For example, the knife developing into the rapier which demanded a high degree of skill and a technique all its own, dwindled away into the infantry officer's parade sword, which in its turn has been abolished and the knife has come back into its own.

Similarly missiles—stone, javelin, dart or those thrown mechanically by sling, catapult, bow or more ponderous engine of war—have served their turn, outstayed their welcome and been relegated to the scrap heap only to be brought back to light and used again in wars separated by centuries of time and immeasurable distances of scientific achievement.

So, in the last war—as again in this—we find primitive weapons bobbing up again and introduced as the latest thing in devices for killing an enemy.

Here are verbatim some passages from an article by me published in the *United Service Magazine* in 1905, as a background to a discussion of our "new" weapons.

* * * *

(Extracts from the *U.S.M.*, 1905):—

... We are still haunted by the ghost of the backdoor bolt in breech actions. By the laying of this ghost ... a series of automatic rifles will appear and an automatic will emerge of perfect mechanism, great accuracy and range and simplicity....

The rifleman will be protected by his shield or his hyposcope and his highly developed intelligence . . . his propellant will be smokeless, invisible, soundless....

The field gun of a year or two ago differed little from its predecessor of centuries before—it recoiled in the same way, was reloaded, relaid and fired again in a precisely similar manner. That gun is already disappearing ... quick-firing field guns—the semi-automatic gun, the automatic gun, the auto-sight—every gun fitted with motor, shield, silencer and methods of courting invisibility.

Great changes in projectiles ... increasing size in proportion to gun ... different natures of charges—smoke-producing material, incendiary, poisonous gases, the use of which we do not yet understand....

The life of guns will be vastly lengthened; liners and partial liners will be carried in the field for repair ... the fortress gun will be a long-range invulnerable machine, lightly poised, automatic, served by a minimum of hands and controlled from the centre of a great spider's web. The position-finding system will continue to develop until we have the complete web with the spider in the middle.... The automobile torpedo, the wirelessly directed torpedo, mines and minefields ever improving; aerial weapons (also on land) . . . kites, aeroplanes, the flying machine controlled by its occupants or from the land ... poisonous gases, smoke-producing explosives, others with stupefying, paralyzing, possible blinding effects we do not yet consider within their scope ... electric lights by night ... blinding and disconcerting tactics ... the era of solitary beams stabbing the darkness will be past....

The gun emplacements will grow less conspicuous, flatter and more uniform with their surroundings . . . the district gunner, with paint pot and brush, exhausting his artistic faculties in colouring the gun and mounting as the giraffe is coloured, as the zebra is striped and assimilating them to the background ... they will all be concealed by art, buried and comparatively safe.

Ever since man understood the use of his hands he has desired and utilized a personal weapon, a club or knife or sword. . . . He will always want it . . . while human nature lasts the *arme blanche* in some form or another is bound to stay with us . . . the train of an army will steadily increase . . . greater provision of ammunition . . . higher rates of expenditure . . . animals will decrease and forage and equipment.

Rations simplified . . . dessicated and concentrated food . . . injections, doping may be resorted to.

Enormous increase in the bulk and weight of ammunition supply . . . transport and supply always greater . . . mechanical traction and transport—the traction engine, motor-car and lorry . . . the pedrail, cross-country motor . . . the automobile capable of moving anywhere without the restrictions of the railroad track . . . the armoured motor-car . . . road car with a machine gun, the road car armoured and gunned, the tortoise-backed cupola-car, armed, invulnerable, swift, unconfined to any road; the battle-car proper, a warship on land . . . little independent cars scouting, holding advanced positions, defending rear-guards . . . cutting-out expeditions, man killing adventures of their own . . . land-ship tactics . . . mining, gun and torpedo attack.

. . . Universal mechanical transport very shortly due (in 1905!) . . . wireless telegraphy and telephones . . . aeroplanes as weapons of offence . . . conflicts in the air, stricken machines falling like great birds . . . tactics of the air . . . the flying ship that can also swim, dive and perambulate. . . .

And all the while . . . we are waiting for the advent of the supreme genius who will, by the production of *the original weapon*, settle the predominance for ages to come.

* * * *

The above is a brief summary of my forecast in 1905, all of which has come to pass, including, further, camouflage, battle dress, dazzle-painting, amphibious tanks and invasion by flat-bottomed craft, high speed coastal vessels and other devices.

All of these have come true, many have appeared and disappeared again, and now in 1942 we are re-inventing ancient devices in a hurry.

Let us now consider team weapons.

The different types of M.G. require intense study and training to ensure mechanical proficiency and collective efficiency. Even that is not enough, a M.G. team is not ready for battle until it has mastered the weapon and has, further, been instructed in the tactical handling of that weapon. That is a subject for specialists and must be learnt in the hard school of routine drudgery and the skilled instruction of qualified specialists. You may know the M.G. inside out and be able to take it down and reassemble it blindfolded and you may have successfully shot off your limited number of rounds, but you are not a qualified machine-gunner until you know how to site your weapon, how to get into and change position, how to husband your resources and to supply ammunition and to get out to come into action in the next best place. Judging by what I have seen at Divisional schools there are many Home Guard machine-gunners who *can* do all that like old Regulars—as indeed many of them are—but the point is that *all* Home Guard machine-gunners must attain this standard before they are satisfied.

Now we come to guns, mortars and (so-called) "projectors," bombards and, may be, sakers, demi-sakers and culverins.

The old differentiation between the types of ordnance is worth repeating. A "gun" was charged with a shot or shell and a certain quantity of powder and depended for its range on the amount of elevation given to the "piece" (i.e., gun-barrel). A "howitzer" was a medium-pace bowler which could vary its range both by varying the charge and also by altering the elevation. Such a weapon can obviously get "plunging" fire on a target with a steep angle of natural features. In short, the gun used to fire "direct" at a target, the howitzer used to go high into the air and come down on it.

The "mortar" was more peculiar. It was generally fixed on a base at a permanent angle (say 45 degrees) and got its variations in range by putting in a bigger or a smaller charge. It was, in fact, a slow lob-bowler. There you have the essential differences—fast, medium and lob.

The modern tendency is to make one weapon do for two purposes, thus we have things called "gun-howitzers" which can "vary their pace" and shoot direct or up in the air. Similarly the mortar has borrowed from the others the variations in elevation and has practically abandoned the use of different charges to obtain different ranges.

The mortar still retains its chief characteristics which are: simplicity, heavy projectile from small weapon and high-angle fire.

It would be out of place to describe any of our mortars in detail, but a very usual type is a light weapon cocked up rigidly at a certain angle with its base resting firmly on the ground. Shells or bombs are dropped in at the muzzle and slide to the breech end, where they fall on a striker.

The projectile contains a bursting change and a fuze to explode it, and also a charge of propellant and a cap to ignite it. That is to say, it is entirely self-contained, and the rate of fire is governed only by the rapidity with which rounds can be popped into the muzzle.

The gun on the other hand is breech-loading, and must have a breech mechanism for opening and closing the breech and also a mechanism for firing the cartridge. The charge may be what is called "fixed ammunition," i.e., completely self-contained, as above, or shell, cartridge and igniter may be loaded separately.

Let us have a look at the Northover Projector. It is by way of being something new, but its prototype was in use on our little ships that defeated the Armada in 1588. Yes, believe it or not, those little smooth-bores were of about the same size as the Northover, had a good type of primitive breech block, were mounted on a swivel and could be "laid" by hand, just like the Northover.

It is a very efficient small gun for firing bombs of any type that will fit its bore. There is only one serious objection to it—its weight. There is no reason why a gun of similar power should not be constructed so that one man could carry it like a handbag, leaving the rest of the team for ammunition and other duties.

We had a very interesting weapon of this sort on experiment in the last war, invented by a marine officer named Bellairs. It is now in the Imperial War Museum. It could be fitted with different kinds of barrel for different kinds of bomb or shell; one group of 5 barrels used to take five Mills grenades apiece (as the Northover could do to-day) if you wanted to do a bit of a scatteration. This mortar was really portable, and there is no reason why the Home Guard should not have one that they could get about with quickly: it also fired bottles filled with appropriate liquid.

One of the most primitive firearms was called a bombard. It was a gun with a small bore for the powder charge and a large bore for the ball or "stone," as it was then. It was strapped down to a solid bed and had no mechanism of any kind. It was fired by a match at the touch-hole and bowled the round shot at the enemy. We have nothing quite so primitive to-day, but it is a curious reversion to type that we actually have weapons which fire projectiles of far greater diameter than the bore of the chamber. For example, the Mills grenade fired from a cup discharger, and the last war football bombs, which had a metal stem sticking out of them which fitted into a very small mortar barrel. The point is that ingenuity suggests from time to time a method of firing a large projectile from a small gun, and one of the weapons is more or less all projectile and no gun on a principle which is only a variant of something very ancient.

Bombs, grenades and mines are a very old story; they tend to become more ingenious, more powerful and more stable as science provides more nearly perfect materials, but every *improvisation* shows a reversion—not to the type recently developed, but to a far earlier type. Thus in the last war and again this we improvise once more the simplest types known to our ancestors—a container filled with whatever we can find in the way of explosive or combustible, a fuse and a match and we throw the damned thing with precisely the same appalling amount of risk as the boarding party in Elizabeth's day or the grenadier at Minden.

Take the thing called a "Fougasse," which is considered up-to-date. It is the earliest form of man-trap devised subsequent to the invention of gunpowder.

It was originally a hole in the ground, or in the rock, dug at such an angle that its discharge would cover the point where one hoped to destroy an enemy. This hole had a charge and means of ignition laid at the bottom and was then filled up with rocks, stones, debris and fragments. It was, in fact, a gun or mortar with a life of one round, as it still is to-day. (Like the male bee, unfortunate representative of the hive.)

(B) INDIRECT FIRE.

Most riflemen are only interested in "aimed fire," that is, shooting at targets which are visible and on which they align their sights more or less deliberately. But the modern practice of firing from the hip, which is not truly "aimed fire," and the issue of various weapons on mountings to the Home Guard, which may in certain circumstances be better employed without actually aiming at the target, justify a few observations by an old gunner on the ways to hit the target even though it is not visible.

The principles of indirect fire are very simple and not new. Without referring to any artillery manuals and without using technical terms which may well have changed since my day, I propose to explain these principles in the hope that the Home Guard may obtain from their weapons "hits on target" when direct fire is impossible.

The circumstances in which indirect methods may be valuable are many and varied—by night, in fog or smoke, firing from behind cover or screened by foliage—how are you to hit men or vehicles, or cover a point that they must pass if you can't see them?

The simplest illustration is with a rifle.

Suppose that your rifle range and butt arrangements are limited to, say, 25 yards, you must put your bullets into that butt at 25 yards, but it may be desirable that you should be aiming at a landscape target which you do not want to spoil. That is to say, you have two targets, one that you aim at and the other where the result of your shots can be recorded. On the indoor range the landscape target is at floor level; you fire at the point indicated on the landscape, but your sights are set at extreme range, so that the bullet will actually hit above the landscape. At the suitable height above the landscape is placed a bull's eye, which is your "sub target"; the height may be decided by calculation or trial and error. You may then go on shooting at indicated points on the landscape and record your accuracy on the sub targets.

This is not a good example of what I mean by "indirect fire," but it illustrates the principle that you can hit with accuracy some point at which you are not actually aiming. You could even cover up your sub target with a paper screen so that it is invisible from the firing point—you are then accurately hitting something you can't see.

Indirect fire is the reverse of this process, but with similar result.

Suppose the Home Guard to have a M.G. or projector or gun or rifle on a fixed mounting in a certain site which covers points that may be worth shooting at when an enemy is likely to be there at a time when you can't actually see him, how do we proceed?

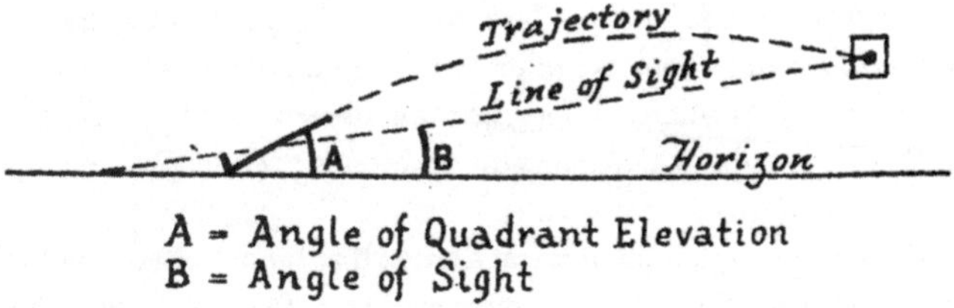

A = Angle of Quadrant Elevation
B = Angle of Sight

Fig. 1.

In daylight we aim the weapon at the point we want to hit with the appropriate elevation and, if we can do so, we fire a few shots to "register" that point—if we cannot fire a few shots we work out the range, and aim the weapon accordingly and then we look around to see how we can make certain of getting the weapon into exactly the same position again so that we can fire blindly with the certainty that our bullets are hitting at that point.

We can do that in a variety of ways. The simplest is to select in the immediate neighbourhood some conspicuous aiming mark that will be visible even if our target is invisible. Suppose, for example, there is a whitewashed wall in front of the weapon (say 25 yards distant) somewhere near the line of fire to the point you hope to put your shots. You "lay" your weapon so that it will hit the target and you make a black conspicuous mark on the white wall and, without altering the position of the weapon, you adjust your sights so that they are aligned on this mark and make a note of the readings on the sights. You then know that, providing the mounting of the gun has not been shifted, all you have to do is to set the sights according to the record and to aim at that black mark and, whatever the conditions of darkness, fog or smoke, your bullets will be hitting the real target though you cannot see it, and you are actually aiming at the black mark.

That can be done for as many targets as are necessary, each with its own aiming mark and the appropriate record of sight adjustment. If it is desired to shoot in darkness each of the aiming marks may be defined by a light—lamp, torch or phosphorus.

Now, suppose it is impracticable to find a convenient white-washed wall—you can put up a stick with a disc on it (called an "aiming post") and aim at that. This is even easier than the mark on the wall because you can stick it up where you like to suit the convenience of the sights instead of having to try to get your sights (whose elevation and deflection are limited) on to a selected mark. The disadvantage of aiming posts is that they may be kicked over, or go cock eye in the wind, and may let you down.

This method is suitable for any weapon on a mounting, but not for a rifle, B.A.R. or light M.G., unless the weapon is fixed in a bed or tripod or other rigid device.

Now suppose you want to fire at a target that cannot be seen from the weapon site at any time. It is in this case necessary to work out two things: (*a*) the line of fire so that the weapon is pointing in the right direction and (*b*) the angle of elevation so as to get the necessary range.

Fig. 1 gives all the definitions we need know.

The weapon is represented by the thing looking like a walking stick with its handle sticking up. The stick represents the barrel and the handle the backsight raised to the necessary height to hit the target, when backsight, foresight and target are all in line, i.e., along the line of sight.

It is clear that the weapon has to be cocked up above the line of sight so as to bring the trajectory of the bullet on to the target. The angle that the barrel makes with the horizontal is called the angle of quadrant elevation or (simply) quadrant angle.

Now it is obvious that if the weapon is pointed in the right direction it may be elevated so as to hit the target equally well by aiming along the sights or (if the target cannot be seen) by cocking up the gun to the proper quadrant angle A. This quadrant angle may be applied by various methods of which one is a clinometer, which consists of a graduated arc and a pendulum (like a plumb-bob) or an instrument embodying a spirit level.

The question now arises—if the target is not visible from the site of the weapon how do we work out the line of fire and the quadrant angle? The line of fire may be plotted on the map and then laid out by compass, but this is liable to be inaccurate. Another way is to get somewhere where you are in line with the gun and the target and plant an aiming post—this may be behind the gun or between it and the target. It is quite obvious that if the gun is aligned on this post it is in the proper line of fire.

Another way would be to get to a high place (roof-top or tree) by the gun and select some prominent feature such as a steeple or chimney which is visible from the gun. Now measure the angle between this prominent feature and the target—it is clear that if the same angle is laid off at the gun the latter is pointing at the target.

The quadrant angle is a little more difficult. The best way is to work out on the rifle range what angles correspond to the different ranges within the scope of the weapon and tabulate these in the form of a range table. If, then, you know the range of the target you apply the appropriate tangent angle and (this is important) *add the angle of sight* in order to lift up the trajectory on to the target.

And that is all there is about it. So long ago as 1908 I worked out methods of indirect fire for machine guns with the M.G. officer of the 1st Rifle Brigade in Malta, and we got excellent results by night. Of course, we were looked upon as daft though the R.A. had already widely adopted indirect fire.

A weapon primarily designed for direct fire will probably give better results that way, but on the other hand if you can't fire direct why not use a little ingenuity and get hits by indirect methods?

If you cannot get in at the front door try the back door.

It is quite certain that we can only do our job with some of the weapons we have by using "Indirect Fire."

CHAPTER VIII.
SIMPLE TACTICS.
(A) Reconnaissance. (B) Patrols. (C) Scouts.
(D) Local Knowledge.

(A) RECONNAISSANCE.

(1) **Reconnaissance** only means going somewhere to find out something of value and reporting it in time to be of use.

(2) Without clear instructions reconnaissance is a waste of time and effort—and often of life.

If going out to reconnoitre you must know:—

    (a) What you are to find out.

    (b) Where you are to go and (possibly) by what route.

    (c) What difficulties in your way are known.

    (d) What you are to do, if interfered with.

    (e) When you are to be back—or to report.

    (f) To whom you are to report and in what form.

(3)   Your report should be:—

    (a) Accurate (**no** guess work).

    (b) Simple (**no** frills).

    (c) Clear (**no** muddle).

    (d) Relevant—*i.e.*, stick to the point, NEVER put in irrelevant details for effect. This is the lowest form of eyewash.

Never over-emphasise a statement, like the West Indian Negro who claimed to be an Englishman on the ground that his father was two Marines.

Some forms of eyewash are very much to be encouraged in military or Home Guard formations, but that is another story for another place. In Reconnaissance Reports the rule is: NO EYEWASH AND NO GUESS-WORK.

(B) PATROLS.

There are three kinds of Infantry Patrol: Fighting, Standing and Reconnoitring.

A Fighting Patrol is sent out for a particular duty or for some special task, *e.g.*, the capture of prisoners for examination, which may require fighting.

A Standing Patrol is sent out to watch important points and approaches or likely enemy landing grounds. It differs from the garrison of a defensive post in that the latter must fight to the last where it is, whereas a Standing Patrol may change position or withdraw.

The following notes apply particularly to Reconnoitring Patrols:—

(1) Day dispositions, even with good fields of fire, are no good by themselves **at night**. They must be supplemented by energetic patrols.

Patrolling needs much practice. Start by day and work up to night work. In the H.G. countrymen, especially those with local knowledge, start with a great advantage.

(2) Patrols must be given a definite route out and return.

(3) Other troops in the vicinity must know what patrols are out, or ordered.

(4) Patrols must be given definite times to return, to be adhered to as closely as possible.

(5) The ideal Patrol is a Commander (leading) 6 men in single file, 2nd in Command at the rear.

(6) Patrols must not split up. Dispersion of small bodies never pays and by night men sent away or dropped behind rarely find their patrol again.

(7) Patrols must be given definite routes **and** objectives. They must keep low, especially on moonlit nights, move in the shadows and take advantage of all cover. Men should be detailed to keep special lookout right, left and behind.

(8) Men must be detailed beforehand as messengers, these are the ones to keep looking back to identify and remember landmarks.

(9) Men must be taught to count **numbers** of hostile parties by sight and sound. They must never **guess**.

(10) The job of a patrol is to collect and send in information and not to fight (unless specifically ordered). The Commander who has sent out the patrol wants to know accurately and promptly **where** the enemy are, **how many** and **what time** observed. This information, however complete, is of no value unless it is got back to be in time to be of use.

(11) All patrols should know of all other patrols they may come across.

(12) Silent movements essential. Best effected by making each step with the heel first followed by the sole of the foot. Using the toes or the whole foot deprives the scout of control of his step. This control is very necessary in wooded areas which are strewn with dead twigs.

(C) SCOUTS.

(1) Scouts are specially trained men who may be employed for reconnaissance or on patrol. But they are very valuable and must not be wasted on routine guard or patrol work if there is something better for them to do.

(2) A Scout can work as a lone hand or in company. He can reconnoitre and report—alone. Or he can carry out a lone task, such as scuppering a post with bombs, or silently killing a sentry.

(3) Preserve your Scouts as a miser hoards his gold.

(4) The best Scouts are gamekeepers, stalkers and poachers—a mixed selection. In the same way you may find God-fearing men amongst Bishops, Bookies and Barmen. The point is that a man with aptitude and opportunity and guts can become a Scout with the necessary training. Encourage the men who are good on patrol, especially if they are used to night work and know the country, to become Scouts.

(5) We require of a Scout certain qualifications:—

    (a) Eye for country.

    (b) Physical fitness. Use of his head, hands and weapons.

    (c) Not afraid of the dark or loneliness.

    (d) Knowledge of his trade, initiative and guts.

(D) LOCAL KNOWLEDGE.

It should be the pride of each man in the H.G. to know the area in which he may be called upon to fight "like the back of his own hand." In agricultural districts most men do know the roads, lanes, gates, stiles, footpaths and the names of all farms and landmarks and so on, but if they do not they should learn the area by day and make sure that they learn it also by night.

Remember, you will very rarely be expected to go far from your own home, or, at any rate, from your own post. You will not be formed up as Companies and Battalions and go marching about in a body—on the contrary, the Platoon is the largest unit ever likely to be concentrated (so far as numbers available permit) and the Sections in that Platoon will most probably be operating in small bodies such as a patrol of 1 and 6, or a post of 3, or even as single Scouts. It is thus obvious how important it is to know your area, particularly by night or in dim light. If you are not country bred, it will be worth your while to suck up information from your comrades who may be gamekeepers or poachers or observers of nature. Or, failing anybody better, somebody like me. They can teach you how invisibility and immobility can form perhaps your best protection—how to dress and how to hide. How to observe and listen—what it means when a jay screams or a cock pheasant shows signs of alarm. They can explain, if you do not know it already, that cattle in a field all gazing intently in one direction indicate some human being or a dog sneaking along that hedge, and that sheep exhibiting signs of alarm are a sure warning to you.

Even the way a dog barks or the flight of a startled thrush may mean something.

*   *   *   *

Learn "fieldcraft" from the many excellent instructors now available. I have been asked to amplify the subject here, but prefer to leave it to them and the official Training Pamphlet. It is a big subject, which should interest many H.G., particularly in rural areas, but it is better studied on the ground than on paper.

CHAPTER IX.
(A) Maps. (B) Compass.

(A) MAPS.
By Major K. M. Hawker, 4 Sussex H.G.

This study is valuable not only to the Home Guard but also to the civilian in times of peace. Let us, therefore, first ask ourselves what a map **means** to us.

Assume that we are using a Gridded Ordnance Survey Map of the scale of one inch to the mile—have one of these in front of you to facilitate study of this subject.

Looking at this map one should imagine he is standing at some given point and, by what the map tells him, visualize the following major points:—

a. How far he can see in each direction.

b. Whether the ground rises or falls in front of him.

c. What general view can be obtained of any water in the neighbourhood.

d. Other likely Observation Posts.

e. Where the surrounding woods and copses lie.

f. The types of local roads, etc.

Questions f and e can be answered by learning the key or legend which appears in the bottom margin at the left of the map. This should be studied and memorized until all the features and conventional signs are instantly recognizable. These are the same on all Ordnance Survey Maps.

Questions a, b, c and d require further study, as they are all dependent on "CONTOURS."

Contours are imaginary lines on the surface of the ground which retain their same height above sea level for their entire length. These are shown on the map by thin red lines running, generally speaking, in all directions over its face. They are graduated in series of fifty feet above datum line (mean sea level) and every two hundred and fifty feet is shown by a heavier red line than the others—thus, the nearer the lines are together the sharper the rise or fall of the ground. For example, take a section of your map showing the part of the country that you know and trace the contour lines, visualizing at the same time how they correspond to the actual ground.

In following a contour line throughout its length numbers will be found at various intervals designating the height above sea level of that particular contour so that, when studying the map and referring to adjacent lines, one can decide whether the ground rises or falls from any given point, also, by comparing the closeness of these lines with the scale on your map, one can approximate the gradient. Therefore, if six consecutively rising contour lines appear within 500 yards one can assume that the rise is fairly steep or 300 feet in 500 yards.

You should be able to find on the map, by means of contours, several examples of the following common features:

Basin.—A piece of level ground surrounded by hills.

Col or Saddle.—A ridge of land connecting two hills lower than the hills it connects but higher than the surrounding terrain.

Defile.—Any feature which causes a body of troops to contract its front. Examples: A pass between two mountains; a bridge, etc.

Gorge.—A deep or rugged ravine.

Spur or Salient.—A projection from the side of a hill departing from the main feature.

Re-Entrant.—The reverse of a spur—the space between two spurs.

Knoll.—A detached hill of no great height.

The Military method of designating a specific point on the map is by "Grid References."

These consist of numbers comprised of **four** or **six** figures, and for the study of this important part of Map Reading use the Gridded Ordnance Survey Map, Sheet 133, "Chichester and Worthing."

The Grid lines run vertically and horizontally over the whole face of the map and every tenth vertical line is marked 20, 40, 50, etc., with every tenth horizontal line in a similar manner, i.e., 20, 30, etc. The intermediate lines, which form the small squares on the map, are numbered in the margin, individually.

In giving a reference the Easterly one is ALWAYS given first and the Northerly one last. This is the fundamental point and MUST be adhered to on every occasion—EAST first then NORTH. Therefore, the Grid reference to the town of LITTLEHAMPTON would be 4621 which interpreted means E. of the 46 vertical and N. of the 21 horizontal, and for STEYNING the reference would be 6130. From this it will be seen that, given a Grid Reference, one mentally divides the numerals in half and reads the first half as 61 E. and the latter as 30 N.

With this method, directions to a given point can be easily indicated, so go one step farther. For example, we wish to indicate by Grid reference the STATION at STEYNING, how do we get to the point INSIDE the square by numbers? We visualise the square 6120 divided again into tenths vertically and horizontally, and estimate by our map that the STATION is 8/10ths E. of the 61 line and 6/10ths N. of the 30 line, which makes our reference in the first case 618 and in the second 306, or the complete one 618306. In the same way the X-roads at FINDON would be 557282 or CHANCTONBURY RING, 575313.

One point which must be emphasised is this—never give a reference of five figures, because you cannot "divide" it to get your verticals or horizontals correct. For example, 45678 might mean 6/10ths E. of the 45 vertical on the 78 horizontal or could just as easily be on the 45 vertical and 8 tenths N. of the 67 horizontal. So, if your point occurs exactly on one line—as does ANNINGTON HILL BARN—give it as 607280, adding the nought to complete the reference. Another example of this is the STATION which appears on the 50 vertical between the 22 and 23 horizontals, which would be referred to as 500223.

The principles of Gridding are very simple, but it is only by constant practising that one can get really fast at giving and plotting references. This should be done at every opportunity until the system becomes "Second Nature."

The Scale will always be found in the bottom margin of the map and the one given in yards is normally used.

The small squares on the map are a kilometre (1,000 metres) square and for all general purposes there are 1,100 yards to a kilometre.

(B) THE COMPASS.

(1) This subject can only be dealt with very briefly here.

Take the same map as before, Gridded Ordnance Survey Map, Sheet 133 also a Protractor, Parallel Rule and Scale (This can be constructed from the Scale in yards appearing in the bottom margin of the map).

(2) The following points must be memorized:—

TRUE NORTH is the direction of the North Pole from the Observer.

GRID NORTH is the direction that the Grid lines point to the top of the map.

MAGNETIC NORTH is the direction in which the compass needle points.

A BEARING is the angle measured clockwise from a fixed line to any other line in question.

MAGNETIC VARIATION is the angle between TRUE N. and MAGNETIC N., which varies from year to year as well as from place to place. This is ALWAYS shown on the right hand margin of the map in terms of the degree of variation with the date, also a note giving the annual increase or decrease of variation so that the current degree can be easily found.

(3) A few primary notes on the Compass follow:—

The Compass is like a clock on its readings.

It has 360 degrees in its complete circumference. A degree is shown thus—360°.

Each degree is divided into 60 minutes, shown 60′.

Each minute has 60 seconds, 60″.

No Compass or Protractor reading can exceed 360° as, after that point is reached, the readings again start from Zero.

In using a Protractor on the Gridded Map an Easterly reading will be obviously less than 180°, and a Westerly reading greater than 180°—Be careful of this in the use of the Protractor.

All the aforementioned points must be thoroughly understood before proceeding further.

(4) For our actual workings we are only interested in the relation between GRID and MAGNETIC Norths so that we may easily convert a bearing from map to compass or vice-versa. In the right hand margin of our map, at the bottom, will be found a diagram showing that in 1928 Mag. N. was 13° 20′ W. of Grid N. It also tells us that the annual decrease is 12′. Therefore, from 1928 to 1940 being twelve years, our present variation is 13° 20′ W. less 12 (years) x 12′, which is 2° 24′, or 10° 56′ W. 1940.

(5) We will now work out the bearing on our map from the OLD WINDMILL at ASHURST, 617352 to the RAILWAY BRIDGE at 636328.

METHOD: Draw a line from OLD WINDMILL through RAILWAY BRIDGE and then, with the protractor CENTRED on OLD WINDMILL and PARALLEL to a vertical Grid line (by means of parallel ruler) measure clockwise the degrees to the line you have just drawn connecting the two points in question. This should read 141° 30′. It is a GRID bearing.

Now, to convert this to a compass bearing we must ADD our Mag. Variation, which is 10° 56′, or for all practical purposes 11° making it 141° 30′ plus 11°, 152° 30′. Inversely, if our compass bearing had been 152° 30′ and we wished to plot it on our map, we should have SUBTRACTED the 11°, making our Grid bearing 141° 30′.

This leads us to a most important finding which is this—If our Magnetic Variation is West our compass bearing is GREATER than our Grid bearing. If the variation is East our compass bearing is LESS than our Grid bearing. Be absolutely SURE of this point, devote time to fixing it in your mind and ALWAYS check yourself until you are quite satisfied that you are right.

(6) We had previously found that the Grid bearing from OLD WINDMILL to RAILWAY BRIDGE was 141° 30′—What is the bearing (Grid) from the RAILWAY BRIDGE to OLD WINDMILL? It is 321° 30′, or 141° 30′ plus 180°. Again the Grid bearing from HILL BARN, 585308 to BUNCTON CHURCH 581332 is 350° (prove this for yourself). What is the bearing from BUNCTON CHURCH to HILL BARN? It is 170°, or 350° less 180°. The conclusions that we draw from this are that:

  a. If the bearing to a given point is LESS than 180° we ADD 180° to find the "Back bearing."

  b. If the bearing to a given point is GREATER than 180° we SUBTRACT 180° to find the "Back bearing."

(7) The Student should, for his own satisfaction and practice, take several Grid bearings on the map which are within easy access of his home, convert them into compass bearings and then go out with a compass and prove his calculations.

(8) One last reminder—Compasses vary and should always be checked whenever possible; if an Easterly or Westerly variation is found in any particular compass it must of course always be taken into consideration with every reading. Also, the presence of iron affects a compass, and care should be exercised, when taking a reading, to keep as far away as possible from all objects that might tend to affect the instrument. The following are minimum safe distances from visible masses of iron:—

       Heavy gun, 60 yards.

Field gun and telegraph wires, 40 yards.

Barbed wire, 10 yards.

Steel helmet, 3 yards.

(9) **Hand Angles**.—Extend the right arm to its fullest extent, forward, fist closed, knuckles upward. The distance between the first and the second knuckles is 3°, the second and third 2°, and the third and fourth 3°, making a total of eight degrees from first to fourth.

With the arm still fully extended, forward, fingers wide apart and hand in as vertical a position as possible, the following angles are approximate:—Tip of little finger to tip of index finger 12°. Tip of little finger to top of thumb, 19°.

The above naturally are only for rough calculations, nevertheless, by checking one's hand with known angles, and knowing one's own hand, one can become exceedingly proficient with this method for general purposes of direction.

CHAPTER X.
FIELD ENGINEERING.
(A) Digging. (B) Sandbags. (C) Obstacles.
(D) Defence of a Village or Locality.

(A) DIGGING.

(1) **Digging.** This sounds formidable, but for the H.G. it is simple. It means—how can I make for myself (or how can we make for the party to which I belong), cover from view and protection from attack, and how can I make the approach of enemy more difficult?

(2) The best protection is **not to be there**—(absence of body is better than presence of mind)—the next best protection is to be invisible and under cover.

It is better to be invisible and reasonably protected from chance shots than to occupy a well constructed fort which is visible from the air and a landmark.

(3) H.G. must learn to take cover so that they are not seen and have reasonable protection against rifles, machine-guns, tanks and air attack.

(4) The first thing to realise is that one rifle-man can find cover and concealment for himself without any digging. If there is a bank, ditch, tree, clump of bushes, milestone or any other ordinary feature at the spot where you have got to do your job there is no engineering to be done.

Example:

In this example there is an ordinary Sussex road and a little rifle-pit dug and sand-bagged by God knows who. You are told to go to that point (a) to observe and report (b) to hold up any doubtful visitors.

My advice is to go to about point A, lie in the ditch, take advantage of concealment and cover and you will be far more comfortable than at B which will attract attackers as jam and beer attract wasps.

The Field Engineering you have done consists in moving away from the place appointed and, if you like, you can stretch a wire across the road close by to catch a cyclist.

(5) In the Manuals of Field Engineering, etc., they tell you how many men, hours, tools, etc., are necessary. In this example it works out at 1 man, 0 time, bayonet or wire-cutters.

This is an appropriate point to emphasize the importance of "cover." This means cover (a) from view, (b) cover from fire—or both. If you are invisible you are almost as safe as protected by cover, but get protection too, if you can.

Always observe and shoot **through** or **round** banks or sandbags, never over the top. A man's head (especially if he moves) is always a good target on a sky-line or over a wall or sandbag. Moreover you should never rest your rifle on solid cover—it appears to steady your aim but actually throws the rifle off the aim. Use cover to get protection but not as a rifle-rest; your forearm or wrist against something solid is the best rifle-rest.

Avoid **obvious** cover; choose something inconspicuous and make it still more inconspicuous by screening it with branches, leaves or a hurdle, etc.

(6) Now suppose you have really got to dig a hole for your protection, there being no convenient ditch or bank or wall. With a pick and shovel an average man can excavate in one hour a yard of Sussex soil, *i.e.*, 3ft. x 3ft. x 3ft., and that is adequate cover for **one man.**

Here is a typical section:—

(N.B. a Weapon-Pit or Rifle-Pit need not necessarily be square; if you are in a hurry scoop it out).

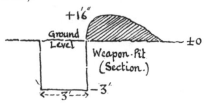

The firing position is more comfortable with an elbow rest about 1ft. 6in. wide.

Note: About 3ft. to 5ft. of earth is proof against rifle-fire. Machine-guns are apt to cut through in time, so always make your parapet as thick as you can.

If you have a hole 3ft. x 3ft. x 3ft. you have got cover for one man, provided you do not let the excavated earth be so conspicuous as to be visible to the enemy and from the air.

(8) Take a yard of earth per man per hour as the standard. If three men are to occupy a post, do it like this:

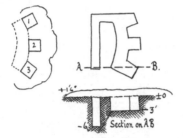

Then if you have time to spare (and surely you will not be attacked within an hour) you make a complete job of it and each of the three men is separated from the others by a "Traverse" (Field Engineering again) which may isolate casualties.

(9) That gives you the nucleus of a fort, or strong point. Now suppose this point is properly "sited," *i.e.*, it covers the ground over which enemy may approach, it is accessible (without being seen) by reliefs, and it is desirable to make it big enough to hold (say) 1 leader and 6 men. In its present state it is fairly snug but very cramped if it is attacked.

(10) Against bombing attack we want more cover. The best cover against bombs is invisibility, the next is reduction of area to the smallest possible dimensions, and the last is overhead cover.

(11) So let us elaborate our three-man trench so as to satisfy these two conditions in their turn.

We dig a slit trench 2ft. 6ins. by 6ft. behind the rifle-pit and separated from it by 3ft. of earth, and join it up at one end with our E-shaped pit.

Now we have got room for three or more riflemen in action and at least four in the best cover that can be made apart from "overhead".

(12) The next stage is "overhead" cover—and that may be left to the H.G. who have dug this pit. Rails, doors, baulks—anything makes the joist structure, after that it is earth and more earth and—never forget it—concealment.

Drain the pit from the lowest point, either by sump or by land-drain in the direction of fall.

Of course, you can make any trench more comfortable by providing a seat, but that is apt to widen the trench unnecessarily. Take your choice—seats are expensive, standing-room free.

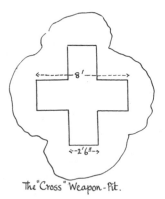

The "Cross" Weapon-Pit.

(13) A good form of rifle or weapon-pit for one to four men is the "Cross-pit."

The dimensions are the standard ones, *i.e.*, about 3ft. x 2½ft. by sufficient depth to give a total of 4ft. 6ins. from floor to top of parapet.

This pit is easy to make and easy to camouflage and it is admirably suited for covering road-junctions or other points where it may become necessary to fire in different directions.

It will be seen that at least three men at a time can fire comfortably in the same direction.

This pit is admirably adapted for throwing bombs from because there is plenty of room for the swing of the arm without danger of bumping the parapet and it has the great merit of being **safe cover from any tank which goes over it.**

The modern tendency is towards slit trenches and no parapet, usually for 2 men. Such tendencies should be treated with discretion.

(B) SANDBAGS.

(1) The sandbag is a useful form of protection if it is properly filled, properly laid and disguised or "camouflaged."

They are sacks measuring 33ins. x 14ins. (empty), they can be filled at the rate of 3 men, 1 sandbag, 1 minute, using ordinary Sussex soil or sand, and shovels. They can be filled at the point where they are required, or, better still, in a sandpit where they may be piled up ready to be taken to wherever required.

It should be filled three-quarters full and then tied with a bow. It is then supposed to be bullet proof against rifles if laid head on,* *i.e.*, "Header"; it is not proof against machine gun fire. Personally I prefer a header and a stretcher, *i.e.*, 30in. AT LEAST.

(2) Sandbags must be laid as bricks are laid by a brick-layer, *i.e.*, properly bonded and with no chinks. Bricks can be laid in a variety of different bonds, *e.g.*, "English" or "Flemish," the essential point is that the bond makes the whole structure into a solid mass which nothing can shake.

Stick to English bond, here it is:—

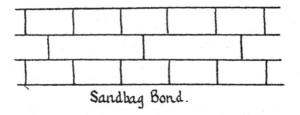

Sandbag Bond.

* Footnote.—Opinions as to what is bullet proof vary enormously. The latest official figures are: Shingle (between boards), 9in.; brick walls, 21in.; sand (in bags), 27in.; sand (loose), 45in.; earth, 60in.; clay, 90in.

A garden wall of good brick, 4½in. thick, will stop a rifle bullet, and then go to pieces after very few rounds. A short burst from a M.G. will go through a 9in. brick wall, so, obviously you are safe if you take cover against odd shots behind walls, etc., which would not stand up to sustained fire; on the other hand, if you want your cover to be proof against sustained fire allow a generous margin.

The best thing to do is to experiment on your rifle range and you will know how much of your particular soil is required.

The top and bottom rows (or "courses) are "headers," *i.e.*, they are laid lengthways towards the front, the intermediate courses are stretchers laid across your front. (Footnote continued on next page.)

(3) When building a parapet or wall lay the bags with the tied up end or the seam INWARDS, the reason being that if they are OUTWARDS very few shots from a M.G. will disembowel them, and when the sand spills out they become useless as protection.

Two sandbags make a pretty good foundation for a loophole for rifles if laid thus:

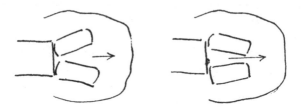

(4) The far greater likelihood of an attacker having to go through a zone of fire if the fire is "converging" or "crossing" instead of "parallel" is illustrated by this diagram:—

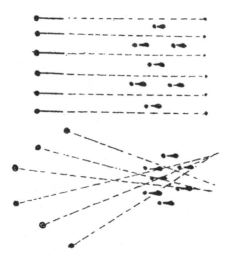

It is to be noted that different rifles have different penetrations; you may be quite happy as to the power of the P17 against an enemy. The penetration of any machine carbine must be very much less.

(5) **Sods.** Sods of rough turf about 18ins. x 9ins. x 5ins. are most valuable for concealment and for revetment (*i.e.*, for a retaining wall). They should be cut with spades from rough ground some distance from the work so as not to give away the position to air observation; they should be laid grass side up.

A Senior Army Officer having inspected a strong point constructed and manned by a Platoon, congratulated the Commander on the work, and said: "I have only one criticism to make—your sods are facing the wrong way."

"That is easily remedied, Sir," said the Platoon Commander. "Platoon—about turn!"

(C) OBSTACLES.

(1) Obstacles are of two kinds, natural and artificial. They must be considered also from both sides—you want obstacles to obstruct the enemy, you also want to be able to get through them if they are in your way.

(2) Natural obstacles are the best because the enemy (let us hope "a stranger in these parts") does not know they are obstacles until he comes upon them. They are streams, swamps, gullies, woods, hedges, ditches, banks, railway embankments and cuttings, fences, etc.

Exploit them all you can without showing them up. You can make many a natural obstacle twice as difficult with a little trouble. For example, a Sussex roadside ditch and hedge is not too easy to scramble through, especially in a hurry (do I know it, shooting at Wiston?), but a few strands of barbed wire woven in will make it a hell of a job for the enemy.

(3) Artificial obstacles range from a solid concrete line of defences down to one strand of wire. They have these points in common: (a) they must be invisible and come as a surprise; (b) their construction must be within your means and the time at your disposal; (c) they must be so sited that they are under your fire and actually do delay the enemy; and (d) they must not be an obstacle to you—or your friends; (d) can be illustrated by referring also to the siting and construction of one of your weapon-pits and strong points.

If this, falling into enemy hands, becomes a thorn in your flesh and gives the enemy an advantage it is probable that it was wrongly conceived, wrongly sited and constructed.

Similarly, if an obstacle designed to delay enemy movement actually **prevents** your movement in the changing conditions of action there is something wrong in its design.

The point is—site all positions and obstacles so that they will help **you** and so that they will not help the enemy if he gets possession of them.

(4) H.G. are not authorised to make permanent obstacles such as solid road-blocks—this being a function of the Engineers working under the orders of the military who may be operating in the area. The reason for this is clear: If we make a solid obstacle in our small locality it might interfere seriously with our own mobile troops wanting to get about in a hurry. But there is no reason why we should not think out how we **could** construct obstacles in emergency, when there are no mobile troops to help us.

There is no reason why H.G. in a village area should not think out a complete scheme for making that village an isolated fortress on a small scale. Having thought out the scheme, make sure that the materials, tools and labour will be available.

(5) Road-blocks, of concrete and rails, built by engineers, are first-class stops for all vehicles, including tanks, but they are no obstacle to men on foot, so the defence of a road-block involves the H.G. in a scheme of improvised defences, including obstacles, around it.

The enemy will only attack a road-block for one purpose—*i.e.*, to give passage to his vehicles. It is, therefore, necessary to defend it in such a way that he cannot reach the block itself in sufficient numbers to dismantle it by hand or to blow it up. This is an example of all-round defence of a post that may be completely isolated. Obviously the H.G. unit responsible for that road block must prepare a ring of obstacles—all under H.G. fire— by wiring and by collecting concertina-wire ready for use, and all other devices that occur to them.

(6) I am a great believer in mouse-traps. There is nothing more satisfactory than to give the enemy a chance to find what looks like chinks in your armour—in fact, to invite him into places where you can, either by converging fire or land-mine, or any other means, give him hell.

Think out your scheme of obstacles NOW, and prepare the necessary measures. When the attack comes it will be too late.

(7) Prepare a scheme NOW for isolated defence of all posts for which you may be responsible, make your H.G. or guardroom, or whatever is the nerve-centre of your unit, impregnable until the last round is fired and the last man is dead.

(8) Prepare NOW for a way out from all defended posts so as to live to fight again. This is not "hedging" nor a direct contradiction to the guiding

principle which should govern fighting by the H.G. It must be obvious to any but a homicidal maniac that circumstances **may** justify our getting away alive rather than remaining dead, but it should be the last resort for H.G. imbued with the right spirit.

(9) The following are **natural obstacles** to medium tanks:—

(a) **Water**—4ft. deep.

(b) **Marshes**—Bogs are fine, but rather scarce.

(c) **Trees**—Diameter not less than 12 inches, spaced less than 8ft. apart.

An old Sussex elm, dropped across a road, might serve.

(d) **Banks. Vertical,** 5ft. high or over. **Sloping,** steeper than 45deg. of length 12ft. or over.

(e) **Ditches.** Gap 12ft. or over.

(10) **Artificial Obstacles:**

(a) **Concrete block and rails** (amply covered by fire).

(b) **Dannert wire.** Three coils will impede a tank, 20 coils are sufficient to stop a tank.

Coils may be laid singly or in pyramids of three coils.

The outer ends of the block are anchored to pickets, and the coils laid across the road in a series of U's. The coils are joined to each other with wire.

Coils of dannert wire laid like bag-nets in groups like this:

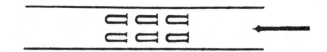

are likely to stop any tank. A heavy tank will go through any amount of taut wire like butter, but a tank going through these bag-nets looks like an Englishman trying to eat spaghetti, and the result is disastrous.

(c) **Anti-Tank Mines.** When these are used they should be laid 3ft. apart. They are placed between rows of wire.

(11) **Cyclist Trap.**—The best trap for a cyclist is a wire stretched across a road about four feet up. If you know enemy cyclists are expected this is what you should do: Select a spot on the road, for preference in a dip and with banks on either side; the spot should be out of sight for some

distance in the direction of the enemy. Now cut a strand of barbed wire loose in the hedge on one side, with your bayonet or tool. Draw the wire across the road and make it fast. Rig several wires if you have time.

(12) Now take cover in the hedge **within a few yards of the trap**. The reason is this: When the cyclist crashes you must leap on him and seize his weapons; he is probably already "out," if not, do the job for him and try to get him and his cycle off the road and hidden. The best warning to a tank is a dead cyclist lying in the road.

(13) If there are several cyclists let them all crash, and shoot or club them individually, starting with those who manage to pull up before crashing.

(14) It is terribly important that we should never catch one of our own cyclists or D.R.'s in a trap—it is a horrible smash at 40 m.p.h. If there are several of our men to spare it is as well to post one some distance away from the trap to shout a warning if our own chaps come along.

(D) DEFENCE OF A VILLAGE OR LOCALITY.

(1) This is a role that may be forced upon a unit of H.G. It is one for which they are very suitable and which they would probably gladly undertake if it is their own village, and the place where their own homes and H.Q. are situated.

(2) The object of such a defence would be to keep the enemy out or prevent him from getting round long enough for mobile troops to come along and mop him up.

(3) The time to arrange for the defence of that village is **NOW**—even though your role is at present an entirely different one.

(4) The defence scheme should be planned in complete detail on paper. These points must be carefully considered: numbers of men available, tools, materials, food, water, ammunition, what road junctions must be covered at all costs—which buildings are strongest, most easily prepared for defence, least conspicuous and least vulnerable from the ground or air.

Each building to be prepared, each posts to be constructed, each weapon pit or obstacle or entanglement must be worked out in men, hours, tools and material.

Alternative positions and obvious dummies must be considered. You may be knocked out of a house by a lucky bomb—but the garden may still be tenable.

(5) Finally a (usually central) "Keep" must be chosen. This might be a group of buildings around our own H.Q., where there are good defensive facilities and observation.

The idea is to make this "Keep" the last point of resistance and the jumping off place for attack to which other detachments might withdraw if actually knocked out of their posts. If possible the "Keep" should dominate the most important point in the village—*e.g.*, a central cross-roads. It is likely that the enemy, before he can tackle the "Keep," may have already been broken up and disorganised, whereas the defending detachments may have actually been formed up into a concentrated tactical unit better able to withstand attack, or to **attack** in their turn, than they were at the beginning.

(6) Learn how to make **bullet proof** sandbag cover and how to reinforce walls, etc. How to make loop-holes, how to make windows and doors defensible, and do not forget fire precautions—the local A.R.P. scheme will probably do this for you.

(7) A wall must be a brick and a half thick to be bullet proof—more for sustained m.g. fire, therefore ordinary garden walls should be reinforced by earth or sandbags.

(8) You can make loopholes in a brick wall with a pickaxe or hammer and chisel. For rifles splay them **on the inside**, for m.g.s **on the outside**. Test the size by aiming a rifle through them in all directions. The idea of the splay is to give you a wide angle of traverse but if a rifle loophole is splayed outwards it may catch a few extra bullets.

(9) Make dummy loopholes all over the place. They will pay hand over fist.

(10) Other points requiring attention are clearing fields of fire, improving communications by making holes and gaps, entanglements, dressing stations and sanitation.

(11) There's a job for the Platoon Commander "in his spare time"!

MANNING SCHEME FOR A VILLAGE AREA.

The Home Guard may be employed in any one of various ways, according to circumstances and the military situation. On a hostile landing from the air the nearest H.G. should report promptly and accurately and try to get within range of one or two hundred yards of the air-borne troops to shoot them before they have time to assemble their equipment or to organise. The first quarter of an hour after the parachutes have descended is of vital importance, because the H.G. would have the advantage of firepower, converging on a concentrated target, whereas after a very short time the enemy will probably have all the advantages, numbers, firepower, mobility and organisation.

It is almost inconceivable that the H.G. could carry out this role unless they are under arms at their posts; it is therefore important to consider the principles which should govern the selection of posts to which the H.G. proceed on the order "action stations."

The fundamental principle is that H.G. should be distributed so that they can effectively carry out any one of their roles; the distribution, moreover, should provide "all round defence in depth" for each of the localities held.

The second principle is that the manning scheme must conform to the strategical or tactical scheme of the Regular Operational Commander. In some cases the H.G. are employed with regulars, in others they may find themselves sometimes or permanently on their own, with no regulars in the vicinity.

Here is an example of the old-fashioned linear defensive system, in depth:

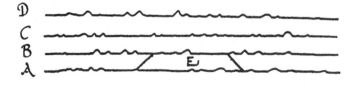

DIAGRAM 1.

A is the coast line or "beach." B, C and D are successive lines prepared and occupied (reading from south to north). All these lines must be ready to face in either direction according to whether attack is coming from the sea or from inland by enemy who have landed from the air and got round.

Attack and penetration are not likely to take place along a continuous defensive line; it is therefore necessary to be able to merge together any two lines of defence as at E.

We must now assume that behind these lines, *i.e.*, to the north, are powerful mobile Regular formations held in leash and ready to be launched in any direction that strategy or higher tactics may dictate.

We can now see what defence in depth means in terms of lines; the depth here is precisely the distance from A to D (or to the ultimate *line* of defence), and that is all.

The H.G. in this area are included in this linear scheme to some extent, if it is only to hold some road blocks embodied in the linear defence systems, but for H.G. the term "all round defence in depth" must have no limitations.

Here is the theory in its simplest terms.

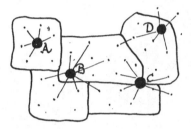

DIAGRAM 2.
(This is not a drawing of five dog biscuits and four spiders, nor a design for stitching a patch-work quilt; it is a serious illustration of the text.)

Here are five parishes or areas each furnishing a section or a platoon or a company. There are four villages or small towns, A, B, C, D, none of them possessing sufficient intrinsic military value for it to be an objective for an attack. Their only value is that they are the geographical points where roads converge, and the enemy cannot get to where he wants to go except by forcing a passage through these or similar villages.

The defensive role of H.G. in these circumstances is to prevent passage by the enemy without hindering our own mobile troops. The H.G. manning scheme must therefore be based on the consideration that the village with its radiating roads is the hub of the system, and the only posts not necessarily embodied in that system are such isolated points, *e.g.* road blocks, as form part of the Regular linear system where it happens to coincide with our area.

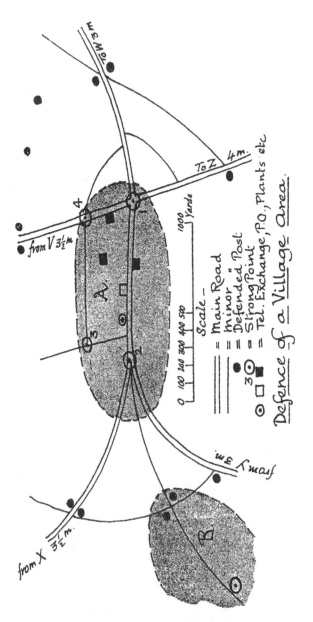

Scale –

0 100 200 300 400 500   1000
⟍ Yards

= Main Road
= Minor „
= Defended Post
= Strong Point
= Tel. Exchange, P.O., Plants etc

Defence of a Village Area.

DIAGRAM 3.

All around A, B, C and D are points (marked with dots) where there is a road junction, or bridge or railway crossing, or some place or building or utility plant it is desired to protect.

Now, if the H.G. unit in that village wishes to approximate to the ideal of "all round defence in depth" they will probably have in the village their H.Q., Battle H.Q., armoury, canteen, picquet room and stores and a really strong point at each of the egresses of the village.

At each of the points marked by a dot they will have an O.P. or a small work to be manned or not, according to circumstances or the number of men available.

If this system is adopted in parishes and spread over the land until not only counties but the whole country is involved, we shall have got all-round defence in depth—the "depth" extending from shore to shore.

The mistake most frequently met with is to take a platoon and to split it up into little packets and distribute them far out, with no reserve, no place to fall back on, and with weak spots all round where enemy penetration would lead to complete collapse.

Here is an example of what I consider the wrong way compared to the right way. It is not an accurate representation of any village, but is typical.

In diagram 3 we have two neighbouring villages. A, compact and built up with the usual array of shops, houses, garage, post office, gas works and other utility plants and small works of value, such as a factory. B is a platoon area with very scattered houses, cottages, farms, etc., with no important roads and no focus of attractions for a hostile landing party, large or small.

Each of these villages supports a platoon of fifty. Company H.Q. is in A, the other two platoons, C and D, are manning works (off the map) in accordance with the military scheme.

A usual sort of layout is for A Platoon to man posts some distance out, marked by black dots, with little or no reserve, and for B to man other posts and keep in reserve the remainder of the platoon somewhere in area B, two or three miles away from A.

This layout is radically unsound, first because A Platoon is squandered too far out, and secondly because B Platoon is being wrongly employed.

The point of view of the men in B Platoon is very widely held and very easy to understand. They say "we enrolled to defend our own homes and we don't see why we should be expected to go away several miles and leave our families and homes unprotected." There is much justice in this, but there being no military objective in this parish they can better protect their homes by going a little further out where they can defend some place which *must* become a hostile objective.

It is an extension of the principle that the way to defend a bridge or road junction is *not* to go and sit on it and be shot to glory, but to arrange defences so that they cover the approaches and bring crossfire to bear on the obstacles, preventing access to the bridge, etc. B Platoon must be persuaded to modify their view.

They would still man the same posts for observation or defence, but their reserve would be moved from some perfectly useless point inside their own parish to the village A at, say, 2. They would there help to build up a reserve for the locality, and it must be remembered that any locality defended on the perimeter and with no reserve has precisely the power of resistance of a meringue.

Similarly if A Platoon withdraws to the far more important points 1 and 4, still maintaining its fan of outposts, but only manning them for observation or defence when circumstances permit, we get this really satisfactory solution.

In village A we have a garrison of Coy. H.Q., and two platoons of 50 each, normally sending out details for observation or patrol and manning the strong points 1, 2 and 4, and either 3 or some other place that is particularly vulnerable or suitable for defence. In these circumstances an attack from the east is held by A Platoon and B Platoon becomes automatically a strong reserve and *vice versa*.

If these principles are sound the immediate task is to make the points 1, 2, 3 and 4 really strong points, properly loopholed, and bagged, wired and protected by road blocks; and to make of that rectangle a miniature fortress wired and protected and prepared for attack from any direction, either by road or cross-country assault. It is much easier to arrange for reliefs, for food and water, and distribution of ammunition and stores, for sanitary services, and for rest and comfort, if the commander has the bulk of his men inside an impenetrable ring and retains the ability to send out reconnoitring, fighting or standing patrols as the situation may demand.

Every individual village or factory or railway centre or other locality must be treated on its own merits, and it is impossible to lay down a theoretical plan to suit them all.

The best we can do is to agree to certain principles of defence and to prepare the work *now*. Once it is decided upon it is a waste of time—and death to the enthusiasm of the H.G.—to go on chopping and changing every time there is a change in the local military command.

Every H.G. Commander, whether responsible for a post or a village or a complete system, should insist on obtaining from his operational Commander the following:—

The plan. Expert advice and help in carrying out the work. Provision of reserve supplies, tools, bombs, grenades, ammunition and stores. Duties connected with Civil Authority, Police, A.R.P., and the inhabitants. If he has seen to these he may rest with a clear conscience; if he has not he has failed in his duty.

To all in responsible positions in the H.G. I say, go and see for yourself. If you require a monument look around, it is either a monument to your patriotism or to your incompetence.

The only time for recovery is the time of preparation—which has almost passed. To anyone whose work is not already done might aptly be said: "Thou fool, tonight thy soul shall be required of thee."

* * * * *

Can we lay down a stereotyped defence for all localities? We cannot. In each locality different conditions and changing circumstances may necessitate departure from a plan devised by experts, especially when successive experts produce a better plan. Commanders cannot all produce out of the same mould a perfect plan, because they all have—let us hope— individual views. One man's meat is another man's poison, or, if you prefer, one man's drink is another man's boisson.

All reasonable men have their own view as to what is a good fighting plan, or what is good administration, or good literature, or music, or even a good dinner.

A man who had been dining out was asked if he had had a good dinner, and he replied, "Well, if the soup had been as hot as the wine, and if the wine had been as old as the chicken, and the chicken had had a breast like the parlourmaid, and the parlourmaid had been as sweet as the savoury, it would have been a pretty good dinner."

Let us leave it at that. We cannot all be Commanders, but we can all be soldiers and do what we are told by men we trust. If in your locality there is a plan and defences to man, and if your orders are clear, go and man your "action stations" and fight like hell, without bothering about whether the plan might not have been better.

CHAPTER XI
AMMUNITION AND EXPLOSIVES.

The subject, "Ammunition and Explosives," is wide and complex, but its ramifications are only for specialists. It is sufficient for the rifleman and the sportsman to take an intelligent interest in the ammunition that they use, but that is not enough for the Home Guard or even for Civil Defence workers, who may become involved in bomb disposal or similar activities.

My object is to cover the ground for the Home Guard in the briefest and simplest way, without needless technicalities. The sporting cartridge is an excellent illustration of many points of the subject. In a section of such a cartridge the following details would be disclosed:

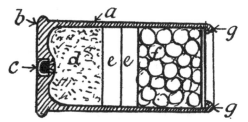

Fig. 1.

(*a*)   Cartridge case. Outer container for all components.
(*b*)   Base and rim. Providing closure against back-blast.
(*c*)   Cap (means of ignition). Containing sensitive explosive.
(*d*)   Charge of powder (propellant).
(*e*)   Wad or wads (gascheck). Insuring full development of expansion.
(*f*)   Load of shot (projectile).
(*g*)   Turnover on wad. Providing closure *forwards*, as at (*e*).

This exemplifies several points common to other forms of ammunition; the words in brackets are the general terms for particular components, and it is slipshod not to use the correct terms. It is important always to use the proper nomenclature in any technical or scientific matter. For example, "calibre" means the diameter of a bore in inches or equivalent measure. It is as idiotic to refer to a gun of "heavy" or "high" calibre as to say a man is six feet old, or a cabbage weighs ninepence.

It is true that in a recent official instruction giving details for disposing of blind high explosive bombs was an injunction not to light with a match lumps of the H.E. "larger than apples," which prompted me to ask, "How big is a piece of coal?" But that is another story; let us emulate the expert who knows what he is talking about and who uses the right words.

Ammunition consists of these elements:—

    The missile (or projectile).
    The machine which propels it.
    The motive power which operates the machine.

This is true of David's sling, the simplest form of artillery. The pebble from the brook is inert until it is put into a sling and propelled by physical agency—David's strong right arm, conditioned by practice.

It is equally true of a 15-in. gun or a mortar or a rifle. Take these things in sequence. The projectile may be a stone or a bullet or a solid shot or an H.E. shell with a complex structure consisting of shell, bursting charge and fuze, the propelling machine may be a sling or catapult or gun, and the motive power may be muscle or air or a propellant charge with some means of ignition.

We can now go on to the next step, which embodies a projectile of a more complicated nature than a load of shot or a bullet. A section of an H.E. shell would show these details:—

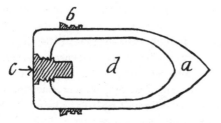

Fig. 2.

(*a*) Shell.
(*b*) Driving band (gascheck).
(*c*) Base fuse (or alternatively, nose fuze).
(*d*) Bursting charge or burster.

A new word has been introduced here, viz., "fuze," meaning the means of ignition of the bursting charge. It may be spelt "fuze" or "fuse"—to try to differentiate would be pedantic.

This part of the subject is rather tricky. Different words are used to name the means of ignition of different kinds of explosive charge, sometimes carried out in stages—e.g., fuze, igniter, "igniter set," detonator, primer. Also different meanings sometimes attach to some of these words; for instance, "fuze," apart from its use as described above, may mean slow or quick match ("safety fuze" and "instantaneous fuze" being the technical names). "Fuze" may have other meanings, but in general it is the means of ignition of a bursting charge in contra-distinction to the means of ignition of a propellant charge; this may be "cap" or "primer" or "tube," but *never* "fuze."

Now let us consider the nature of explosives. Explosion means combustion so rapid as to produce gases of sufficient expansive strength to act as a propellant or as disruptive agent.

"Detonation" means combustion so rapid as to produce a practically instantaneous explosion. Such an explosive is too rapid and too violent to be controlled, and therefore cannot be used as a propellant; the general name for such explosives is High Explosive, or H.E.

Gunpowder is the oldest, simplest, most stable and most easily handled of all explosives. It is a purely mechanical mixture of powdered willow charcoal, sulphur and saltpetre in certain proportions which have been found by experiment to be most suitable (approximately 15:10:75).

It is dry mixture which when ignited burns rapidly and produces a large volume of gases. If it is spread in the open it simply burns from the point of ignition to the further side and its rate of burning can be observed. If, however, it is confined the rapidity of combustion is greatly increased and the expansive force more fully developed.

It can, therefore, be used as a propellant or as disruptive agent. If used as a propellant it is clear that the length of gun barrel should be such that the whole of the powder charge is consumed during the passage of the projectile to the muzzle, or the other way round. That is to say, the rate of burning and the length of barrel have a quite definite relationship.

If used as a disruptive agent gunpowder must be "tamped," i.e., confined so that its violence is increased. It has the peculiarity that when ignited the explosion takes the line of least resistance. If, for example, it is desired to blow a hole in a wall and the powder is put in a bag against the wall the explosion will waste its sweetness on the desert air and the wall will remain intact. If, however, the powder is "tamped" so heavily by piling rocks and earth on it that the wall offers an easy way out the wall will be breached.

The mixture in its primitive form is not used nowadays. It is very susceptible to moisture ("Trust God, but keep your powder dry") and is treated in manufacture in different ways, so that it assumes a granular character, the grains being of all sizes from fine pistol powder up through various grades known as "Pebble," culminating in the hexagonal lumps known as "Prism" powder, so large as to require fitting together by hand in the cartridge case for a heavy gun. Grained powders are usually highly polished with graphite or similar material.

This is the prototype of all propellants which have developed within living memory into an infinite variety with every variation of quickness, punch and power.

Sportsmen will remember, of course, many sporting powders—"E.C., Schultze, Smokeless Diamond, Ballistite, etc.," each with its own characteristic colour and form of grain. These powders are of different groups, e.g., "Nitro"; similarly service cartridges may contain cordite or an American pyro-cellulose powder or even "ballistite" for grenade dischargers. This ballistite is a very powerful powder with a terrific punch, and is therefore suitable for grenades, though it has fallen into disfavour with sportsmen (I suspect that a scientist would tell you that ballistite is, in fact, both a propellant *and* a high explosive).

So much for propellants. They all have one characteristic in common which is not the case with all H.E., and that is their stability and lack of sensitiveness to shock or jolting. At the same time other characteristics require careful watching according to their purpose and the climatic conditions where they are to be used; for example, in a country liable to extremes of temperature it may be advisable to use a more consistent powder than one more powerful, but less stable, which might be ideal in a temperate climate.

And now for high explosives. These are not exactly a "mixture" like gunpowder, but are in the nature of a chemical combination which when exploded or detonated again undergoes a chemical change in producing the gases of expansion. They may be chemical combinations with certain "admixtures."

The simplest is perhaps guncotton, which is made by acting upon cotton or wood fibre with sulphuric and nitric acids. This is a very powerful explosive and very easy and safe to handle if kept damped with acid solution (dilute Phenol).

It is formed into slabs like small bricks. In each slab is a circular hole into which a dry guncotton "primer" is inserted when it is required to use the slab; in the primer is inserted a "detonator," which is a small tube containing a highly sensitive explosive composition. The slab or slabs are laid in contact with what is required to disrupt and the detonator is prepared for firing either by electricity or by a length of quick and slow match (so called "instantaneous" and "safety fuze").

The action is that the detonator actually *detonates* the dry primer; i.e., it brings about an instantaneous explosion as opposed to the comparatively slow combustion of guncotton if ignited. In its turn the primer, being in contact with the wet slab, brings about simultaneously with its own detonation a similar detonation in the whole mass of guncotton.

H.E. has the characteristic that its sudden and violent effect acts in the line of *greatest* resistance, so that contact with the dud shell insures that the detonation will all take effect against the shell and not against "the desert air." Thus you can cut through a tree, as with a saw, by stringing round it a "necklace" of guncotton primers and detonating them.

One other point of interest is the sympathy of similar explosives; for instance, four 73 grenades were placed at intervals of about 2 ft. The first in the line was exploded by means of a safety fuze. The explosion which followed appeared as one and not four. It may be, of course, that there is a period between each explosion, but if there is it is so short that it is undetected by the human ear. When such a disaster occurs as the blowing up of the battleship "Hood" it may be that this colossal detonation may have had its origin in a minor explosion. This sort of experience might encourage all Home Guard to handle all explosives with greater care than they might use if not warned.

For the love of Mike never tell anybody to "detonate" a Mills grenade, meaning that he is to "prime" it by inserting the "ignition Set." It is an old misuse of language and if the man so instructed only knows the meaning of words and does not realise that the order is given by a man who does not know the meaning of words he will either (*a*) use a demolition set and blow the grenade up or (*b*) pull out the safety pin and throw the grenade, which will then in the course of nature be detonated after the appointed number of seconds.

This is rather reminiscent of an unpopular major in the last war whose tired horse stumbled, and he got off and kicked it in the belly and said to his groom, "Take this XX!—x! horse to the farrier and have him shod." Next day he asked, "Where's my, etc., horse?" And the man replied, "The farrier, as ordered, shot that horse last night." That groom if told to have the horse "shoed" would have had him shod, but "shod" to him meant "shot."

The technical terminology is certainly confusing, but if we always use the official words we will go wrong less often. To "fuze" a shell or bomb or mine means to insert the "fuze." To "prime" means to insert the primer and sometimes to insert primer *and* detonator, or "igniter set" as in the case of the Mills grenade.

To get back to H.E. Nitro-glycerin is a combination of nitric acid and glycerin. This is a very dangerous and unstable liquid liable to explosion or detonation on the slightest provocation. To make it more stable it is soaked up in siliceous earth (called Kieselguhr, if you can bear a German word) in the same way that water can be soaked up and made portable in a sponge. This portable nitro-glycerin is called dynamite and there are various forms of H.E. made easier to handle in this manner.

There are other forms of H.E., such as T.N.T., ammonal, Lyddite (which is Picric acid), etc., whose constituents are only of interest to the chemist, but all of which should be treated with great respect by us H.G.'s who need not know what is their composition so long as we know their use and the precautions for their handling and storage.

All of these forms of H.E. require to be provided with an appropriate primer, fuze or detonator which will assure true detonation as opposed to combustion or explosion.

There is another word of which we must understand the meaning. When a shell or bomb, etc., has been fuzed or primed or whatever is the process in that particular case there is sometimes a final step by which the fuze is made operative. This is the step when the last remaining safety precaution is removed so that the H.E. is ready to function. It is rather like the removal from a ship on the slipway of all props and chocks so that a push will launch the vessel on its journey. This process is called "arming." The safety precaution may be a safety pin or a mechanical device to prevent unintentional explosion, when you remove the safety pin or make the device operative the fuze or whatever is the means of detonating the explosive is said to be "armed."

This statement is open to correction by experts. I understand that in certain schools, for example, a Mills grenade is said to be "armed" when the igniter set is inserted (commonly known officially as "priming the grenade"), but I think that is merely an instance of terminological inexactitude which makes everything so much more difficult for the seeker after knowledge.

I have carefully avoided detailed reference to any particular one of the almost countless types of ammunition and explosives that the H.G. have to handle and in conclusion I offer a few general remarks on storage, care and maintenance by the Home Guard.

Each Company has had ammunition stores constructed mostly to a design which is not equally satisfactory in all localities. In these stores are collected many and varied types of material.

In my opinion the following are some of the principles which should guide battalion, company and platoon commanders in their stewardship of what is of great importance to the fighting efficiency of the H.G.

(1) In each battalion, company and platoon there should be one specialist (with an understudy) to take charge of all explosives.

In the battalion it is the "Ammunition Officer," in the company it should be an officer or N.C.O. of experience with sufficient time and knowledge to take on the job in addition to his company duties; in the platoon it should be a man who is capable of acting as storeman. It is very important to have all the different natures of ammunition properly arranged and stacked and exact tally kept of all receipts and issues. Any storekeeper, cellarman or tradesman will know how to do this job.

In each store should be an inventory board with a stock sheet kept up to date. Each separate lot of ammunition of each nature should have something like a "bin card" kept up to date and the bin cards should be checked periodically against the stock sheet and actual stock.

(2) In each store should be a board with clear instructions for arrangement of storage, safety precautions, and orders as to how to report and deal with any observed deterioration or other change in condition.

Inside every door should be pinned up the Army Form G953,

"Regulations for Explosives Storehouses Generally." A thermometer is advisable. Who will pay for it? If I had an ammunition store to look after I would buy the thermometer myself and put the cost of it in the account of all the things Home Guard do without hope of repayment.

(3) The store, whether well or badly designed, should be made proof against extremes of temperature, camouflaged, shielded from sun and observation, ventilated and kept in apple-pie order. You will not get this done by higher authority—do it yourself and do it NOW.

Footnote.—The R.N. and R.A. pay the most careful attention to the conditions under which their ammunition is stored because they know that extremes of temperature (even if not dangerous) will play the deuce with accuracy. As an illustration of what can happen in extremes of heat here is a table showing the average "life" of explosives stored at the temperatures shown:—

Ratio of Temperature Depreciation.

70	deg.	F.	...	...	...	30	years
80	,,	,,	...	...	...	19	,,
90	,,	,,	...	...	...	9	,,
140	,,	,,	...	...	...	200	days
180	,,	,,	...	...	...	17	,,

(These figures are unofficial and relate to unspecified forms of explosive. They are, however, illuminating.)

Why do I think it necessary to stress the importance of learning something about explosives?

For the rifleman or sportsman the answer is easy. He will get better results if he understands the things he is using. He will improve his performance and kill more cleanly.

For the H.G. the answer is easier still. The H.G. exist for one purpose only—to kill boches, if they come, with promptitude and despatch. If you know your weapons and ammunition you will be able to do so, if you do not the boche will kill you.

Every boche wants to die for his Führer—it would be the height of inhospitality not to oblige him.

CHAPTER XII.
TANKS, DIVE BOMBERS AND PARACHUTISTS.

The following notes have been compiled from a variety of sources.

(1) **Tanks and Dive Bombers** have certain points in common; for example they are absolutely terrifying to the bravest men until such men become acclimatised. They are also both largely used as a special kind of artillery—*i.e.*, to produce at close quarters the effect of heavy bombardment. Again, they suffer from certain inherent weaknesses, which only experience of their action can teach us.

(2) The reply to these attacks is a combination of concealment, cover, reserving of fire and bomb attack till at short range—and above all—guts.

It is easy to talk sitting on one's backside in a comfortable chair. It is so hard to put into practice what we know is right.

(3) The essence of the thing is that when dive bombed we pay no attention at all until the bomber is on top of our sights and we then let him have it at point-blank. With the tank we must learn that we are safest from the tank when we are so close that we can climb on to him and pop a Mills grenade in at the top or shoot one of the crew through a slit.

(4) The tank is a terror at 200 yards—it is the poor blind beggar when you can touch it.

(5) **Taking cover under air attack.** In dive bombing you must carry on as though there were no dive bombing going on—it is very frightening but nothing like as dangerous as it sounds. If it makes you get your head under cover it will have served its purpose—so do not put your head down.

In case of attack from the air the rules are: —(a) scatter, (b) lie down and keep still, (c) **never look up**—the human upturned face is like a heliograph—as any wood pigeon would tell you, (d) cover your neck with your arms and go on looking to your front.

INSTRUCTIONS WHEN **NOT** UNDER DIRECT MILITARY ORDERS.

1. Dive bombers travel at more than 350 m.p.h., therefore SPEED IS ESSENTIAL.
2. The moment that bombs start to fall in the vicinity—GET UNDER COVER.
3. Any cover is better than none, *e.g.*:
   (a) If you are in a building—STAY THERE.

(b)   If you are on a road and it has a ditch beside it—GET INTO IT.

(c)   If you are in a town and the street has a gutter—LIE DOWN IN IT.

In fact, flatten yourself behind anything that will deflect the blast of the bomb so that it passes over you.

4.   If you are caught in the open, do not panic, DO NOT START RUNNING, instead:—

(a)   Throw yourself face downwards on the ground.

(b)   Rest the weight of your body upon your elbows (which act as shock absorbers).

(c)   With your elbows on the ground place your hands so that the fingers of both hands interlace across the nape of the neck, your arms cover the ears.

(d)   KEEP YOUR MOUTH SHUT.

(e)   DO NOT CLENCH YOUR TEETH.

The reason for:—

(a)   is to avoid splinters and especially blast.

(b)   is to avoid being winded by the concussion.

(c)   is to prevent the blast from damaging the eardrums and jerking the head back, thus possibly injuring the spine.

(d)   is to prevent unwanted air being forced into the lungs.

(e)   is to prevent the concussion jerking the teeth together.

5.   It would be minutes well spent to practice adopting this attitude suddenly whenever you think of it.

6.   If you follow the above instructions, unless a bomb lands almost on top of you, you stand a very good chance of surviving a bombing raid.

7.   THIS SHOULD GIVE YOU CONFIDENCE BECAUSE A BOMB CAN FALL WITHIN TWENTY YARDS OF YOUR PROSTRATE FIGURE WITHOUT HURTING YOU.

(6)   **Enemy Parachutists.**—Single parachutists may be friendly pilots, or Germans who have baled out. They must be immediately secured, but not attacked unless they show fight or try to escape. A parachutist speaking broken English may be one of our Polish or Czech allies, so do not regard such a man as definitely hostile.

It may be assumed that any party of parachutists over six in number is hostile and should be attacked at once.

CHAPTER XIII.
ATTACK.

It is now time to clear our minds about the various facets of our "Role" as H.G.

It will be realised that our role of observation and report may involve the definite duty of NOT FIGHTING.

Again, our duty of resistance and delaying action may make it imperative to fight a bit and yield a bit.

In the defence of a pit or post or locality it may be better to fight and **get out**, so as to fight again.

Circumstances may, however, dictate that we must stay where we are and fight to the last round.

Here follow, verbatim, the views of an experienced Instructor of the aggressive school (and we could do with a lot of them). I agree completely with them in principle and only jib at the difficulty of literally cutting out the word "defence" from our vocabulary. After all, he has had to use this objectionable word in the title of his paper, and he is compelled to use the still more loathsome expression "Static Defence."

"Static Defence" can only be applied to an inanimate break-water or concrete road-block—not to **men**.

A horrible new term "Static observation" can surely only be applied to the fixed glassy gaze of Dr. Crippen, and other celebrities, in effigy at Mme. Tussaud's.

I found this new expression, "static," so frequently that I looked it up in the dictionary,—it says nothing about "static defencia," but it does give "*static ataxia*, inability to stand without falling or staggering." Let those that enjoy it have it.

With this reservation let us study what our Instructor says, it deserves the most careful consideration.

ATTACK.
By Capt. C READ THOMPSON, Wisborough Green H.G.
"ATTACK IS THE BEST MEANS OF DEFENCE."

A truism—yet many individuals and nations seem to have overlooked it in the last few years.

Belgium, Holland, Norway, Denmark—they all mistakenly believed that a system of passive defence would best protect their interests. France based her war plans on defence.

And the Home Guards?

"Guards." "Defence Volunteers!" "Your duty is to observe rather than fight." "Help to defend your homes."

It would indeed be surprising if the Home Guards were still unaffected by this paralysing blight of "defence."

Yet no boxer will win a fight if, during training, it has been drilled into him that warding off blows is his main object.

No military organisation can hope for success unless, deep bitten into their consciousness, is the realisation that their only job in life is not to defend themselves and their homes, but utterly to destroy the enemy on every possible occasion and by any and every means in their power.

"Attack—attack—and then attack again!"

That should be the spirit animating the Home Guards—the guiding principle behind all their training.

Not only is this "offensive spirit" correct psychologically, but it is sound common sense from a military standpoint.

Static defence under modern conditions is a highly scientific problem calling for expert knowledge and long careful planning. Defence by retirement is one of the most difficult operations troops can be called upon to perform.

The Home Guards have neither the training, weapons nor leadership to conduct successfully a static defence. As semi-trained, poorly equipped troops their only chance of success is to defend by a constant series of harrying attacks. Attacks that are unexpected and unorthodox. Attacks that are only broken off for the purpose of finding a fresh position from which to attack again.

But—and this is vital—to attack successfully troops must be imbued with the offensive spirit. It must be part of their very being.

How are we to inculcate in the Home Guards this "spirit of attack?"

To begin with, we should cut out the word "defence" from our vocabulary.

We should never refer to trenches as "defensive positions." Trenches are places from which an attack can be made on the enemy.

Never suggest to men on guard duty that they are there for the purpose of "defending" or "protecting" a post. They are an attacking force whose duty it is to surprise and scupper enemy intruders.

Let it be known that the "retreat" from Dunkirk—like every other successful retreat—was, in reality, a constant series of fierce counter-attacks.

Impress on everyone that the tank is not some mechanical monstrosity to be regarded with awe. Tanks are very vulnerable moving forts garrisoned by a few half blind, dazed and very apprehensive men; men who are effective only against defence and soon become demoralised when faced by a few resolute attackers who know their job.

Above all, never suggest that we are a body of troops anxiously preparing to ward off some terrifying blow.

The Home Guards are an attacking force lying in wait for, and ready to destroy, any enemy who dares to set foot on our shores.

We are the hunters—not the hunted.

TRAINING FOR ATTACK

There is a distinct danger in the fact that most of the training of the Home Guards is conducted by ex-officers of the last war.

Such officers were brought up under a system which allowed little scope for individual initiative. Their job was merely to carry out a well tested, long established system of training which was designed to produce large units of highly disciplined men capable of carrying out large group movements with precision and blind obedience.

In the Home Guard, Commanders are faced with an entirely different proposition.

Firstly, there is no recognised system of training. This means that the efficiency of the men will be in direct ratio to the individual initiative and instructional ability of their officers.

Secondly, instead of turning out large disciplined units, the aim of Home Guard training should be to produce a number of individuals each possessing (to quote General Wavell) the qualities of "a successful poacher, cat burglar and gunman." Men trained to think and act for, and, if necessary, by themselves.

Home Guard leaders should recognise this difference in aims. They should avoid the danger of mistaking smartness for efficiency. Training should be based on common sense and fitness for a particular purpose rather than on a Drill Manual.

It is suggested therefore that after the recruit has learnt the A.B.C. of his job—that is, to handle his arms in a workmanlike manner and to recognise and perform elementary military terms and movements—the majority of his training should be confined to the following:—

(1) **Use of the rifle as an offensive weapon.**

This does not mean being able to blaze off a large number of loosely aimed shots in a short time. Neither does it mean the ability to score a number of bulls with slow deliberate shots. The rifle only becomes an offensive weapon when the user can snapshot at a moving or half hidden target from any position and with reasonable accuracy. The Home Guard rifle is for sniping and harrying, not for defence.

(2) **Use of cover in attack.**

It is almost certain that for some time to come the Home Guard will be outclassed by the enemy in the matter of offensive weapons. The only means to offset this superior striking power is by the extensive use of cover. Ambushes, surprise raids and sniping must be the order of the day. Houses, ditches, dead ground and hedges—these will be the "communication trenches" of the Home Guards—the means by which they may get within striking distance of the enemy.

(3) **Passing Information.**

In view of the fact that the Home Guards possess few trained signallers and will probably fight in small scattered groups against a highly mobile enemy, the question of their getting information back to H.Q. is of great importance.

They should be well drilled and have extensive practice in—"What to report—How to report—Who to report to."

They should be taught to use standard message forms and abbreviations and never to rely on verbal communications.

Above all it should be instilled into them that no information is of any use unless it is transmitted with speed and accuracy.

(4) **Guard Duties.**

Guard duties of various kinds may, in the future, prove to be one of the most onerous tasks the Home Guard are asked to perform. It is essential, therefore, that all men be so trained that they thoroughly understand and act upon the following:—

(a)   Guards are an attacking, not a defensive force.

(b)   Their main duty is not merely to defend their post or protect themselves but to defeat, and render harmless, enemy intruders.

(c)   Guards should assume that everyone without exception is an enemy until he has been proved to be a friend.

(d)   They should be ready at all times to take the initiative against anyone approaching their post.

(e)   Guards should so dispose themselves that it is the intruder who is surprised—never the guard.

(5) **Attacking Tactics.**

As previously stated, the attacking methods of Home Guards must be based on ambushes, raids and harrying tactics, all of which depend for success on the individual initiative of small groups of men.

It is suggested, therefore, that the following maxims be kept in mind when training men for this type of warfare:—

(a)   Never prepare an elaborate scheme depending on close direction and co-operation. It is far better merely to give the men a general idea of what they are expected to achieve and let them learn by experience and examination of their own mistakes.

(b)   Train the men in "acting the enemy." In a tactical exercise, let them be the advancing invaders as well as the attacking Home Guards. This will teach them the art of anticipating probable enemy action.

(c)   Never refer to "retreat" or "retirement." Every foot of the country is "front line" if, from it, one can make contact with the enemy. Home Guards, when forced from advance positions, take up "secondary offensive positions."

(d)   Train the men to avoid the obvious in attack. Nothing so upsets an advancing force as being kept guessing. A few shots from an unexpected quarter are far more demoralising than a heavy volume of fire from an obvious position.

CHAPTER XIV.
COMMUNICATIONS.

(1) **Means.** Wireless. Telephone. Written message conveyed by car, bicycle or runner. Verbal message. Pigeons.

These different methods have these points in common:

(a) It must be clear who from and to whom, what the information is (clear, concise and complete), and at what time the subject of the message occurred and what time the message was sent.

(b) A standard message form must always be used. For preference the Service Form (Army Form C2128) which is the result of years of experience and which is the only form Army Signals will accept.

A Commander may, of course, adopt a simpler form for domestic use, *e.g.*, from an observation post to the Section H.Q., but it is advisable to stick to the accepted sequence. The following standing order should be posted up in every observation post, alarm post, H.Q. and guardroom:

"Every H.G. detailed for communication by telephone or any other means will give the following information in the following order:
Four W's.

    (a)   Who he is and name of his post and the section to which he belongs.

    (b)   What he saw (or heard).

    (c)   Where he saw it.

    (d)   What time he saw it.

This must be learnt by heart by every member."

(2) **Intercommunication between H.G., the Military, Police and Civil Defence Services.**—Until an emergency exists Home Guards are not on duty by day, therefore, detailed inter-communication arrangements cannot be made, but every Battalion, Company and Platoon H.Q. should be accessible by day and night by telephone and by D.R. (despatch rider, or messenger). There is, therefore, the framework for an intercommunication system.

By night in normal times and **night and day during emergency**, communication must be established between H.G., the Military, the Police and other Civil Defence Services.

In view of the probable breakdown of telephones on an emergency, in every unit a complete system of communication by car, bicycle or runner must be organised **and continually practised.**

(3) The question of priority for a H.G. post or patrol reporting enemy activity does not arise. They report to the Section or Platoon which has posted them.

Obviously the Section or Platoon must get the news to Company H.Q. as soon as possible, but equally obviously if there is a military unit in the immediate vicinity it should also be informed.

(4) The question of priority for a H.G. Company Headquarters reporting enemy activity will be settled by the Military Commander on the spot, if there is one—in all other cases the sequence will be as follows:—

Inform: (1) The Police.
          (2) Your Battalion H.Q.
          (3) Your neighbouring Companies.

(5)   The Service Message Form (Army Form C2128) must always be used when working with Regular Troops or Signal Service. There are two reasons: (a) It is a far better form than any untechnical officer can design for himself. (b) Signals will always accept for transmission the Service Message form but they will not look at a private one.

This applies to Battalion and Coy. H.Q.—but it is better to use a standard Form, which is simple, for communication between (say) an Observation Post and the Patrol or Section Leader.

(6) In sending messages, avoid, if possible, mixing up two subjects in the same message. A historic example was a message from Kitchener sent up the Nile at the time when the "Buzzer" was first introduced into the Signal Service. His message was "Where is Lieutenant Wilson, A.A.A. How is the buzzer working?" The reply was that the officer was at such and such a place and that his work was giving satisfaction.

(7) **Communication with Police.** Speaking generally, the best person for any individual member of the H.G. to report to if he has information on any subject whatsoever is his Leader or Commander **if he is immediately accessible**, otherwise the nearest Constable or Police Station. (This is an invariable rule, unless you are cheek by jowl with a military unit—in that case you must tell them first and then the Police).

The reason for reporting to the Police first is that each Police Station has up-to-date information as to the distribution of Military, H.G., and Civil Defence Services in the neighbourhood and can pass on reports to those concerned and can put the nearest military unit in action without delay.

During Emergency, Battalion Commanders will detail members of the H.G. to be stationed at Divisional and Sub-Divisional Police Stations ready to take messages to units of the H.G. They are also responsible for distributing information to their own Companies.

(8) **Signalling.** This subject appears to me to excite so little enthusiasm in the H.G. that it would be a waste of space to include it in this book.

It is quite possible to learn simple Morse (visual and by sound) and/or Semaphore in a very short period of concentrated study, but H.G. who are not old signallers do not appear to take kindly to it. A man who knows it is an asset to his unit. BUT ONLY IF THE OTHER PEOPLE KNOW IT TOO.

As in everything else the circumstances differ in each Battalion and Company. Their needs also differ. Some of them have admirable systems of communication. All units requiring advice and technical assistance cannot do better than consult the nearest G.P.O. Battalion of H.G.

For the moment I will leave it at that—if men want to learn to be signallers it is the easiest class to arrange, provided you have got one old Navy or Army signaller to teach and a Boy Scouts' manual, but *signalling comes after the weapons in importance.*

It is no good trying to master everything at once; first things first. There is a moral in the story of the burglar and the baby. The burglar, having difficulty with the window of the night nursery, tapped on the pane and said, "Be a pal, kid, and help me with this latch," and the baby said, "Don't be so damned silly, I can't walk yet."

NOTES ON THE EMPLOYMENT OF PIGEONS IN THE HOME GUARD.

By Lt. L. W. Maddock, Group Pigeon Officer,
Berkshire H.G.

Advantages. The H.G. being a static force it is possible to make use of established pigeon lofts.

Pigeons can travel at high speed and are unaffected by the nature of the ground.

Pigeons cannot talk and, if captured, will not give away their origin or destination. This is an advantage over all other means of communication. Even the wireless has its wave-length.

They can carry messages and sketches.

They can pass over a gassed or heavily shelled area.

They can travel long distances.

Disadvantages. Their flight is adversely affected by bad weather conditions. They have difficulty in finding their way in fog.

They will not fly in the dark unless specially trained.

Pigeons should not be kept away from their loft for more than 4-5 days.

The number of birds available is usually limited and their supply to forward units a matter of difficulty.

(*Note*:—It will be observed that most of these disadvantages do not apply to the use of pigeons in the H.G.)

Establishing a Pigeon Service. When a Home Guard unit contemplates employing pigeons as a means of communication the idea usually emanates from someone who has already had some experience of the matter. If not, it should be ascertained as soon as possible whether there is a volunteer in the unit who is a pigeon fancier. His knowledge and experience may be invaluable. If it is found that there are several, so much the better.

Whether the unit contains an experienced pigeoneer or not, it will be necessary for contact to be made with (1) the Group Pigeon Officer, or if none exists, the Command Pigeon Officer, through the usual channels, and (2) the National Pigeon Service.

The Group Pigeon Officer. This officer is responsible for all Home Guard pigeon services within the area covered by Group H.Q. Even if the pigeon service is a local one only it is important that no use of pigeons is made without his acquiescence and it is not possible to obtain official equipment except through him. There are many other reasons why nothing should be done without his co-operation.

The National Pigeon Service. This organisation was brought into being some months before the outbreak of the present war. Its members are pigeon fanciers who have offered the use of their lofts and birds to the Services. They have also undertaken to breed young birds for the exclusive use of the Services. As there are some thousands of N.P.S. members and their lofts are spread over the whole country it is probable that there is at least one within the area of your unit who will be of assistance and, if so, you will be spread the trouble of establishing a new loft—a lengthy business anyway.

One N.P.S. member in each district has been appointed P.S.O. (Pigeon Supply Officer) and it is through him that contact should be made with individual members. The address of your nearest P.S.O. and any other information regarding the N.P.S. can be obtained from the Secretary, Mr. J. Selby-Thomas, 22, Clarence St., Gloucester.

Equipment. The following equipment can be obtained through your Group Pigeon Officer:—

S type Baskets (20-bird).

D type Baskets (these vary slightly in size but will take 6-10 birds).

T type Baskets (2 bird).

Drinking troughs.

Message Carriers and Rings.

Books of Message Forms (Army Book 418B).

Pads of Carrier's Notes for Conveyance of Live Pigeons (A.M. Form 1584).

Pads of Consignment Notes (Army Form G988).

Labels for Baskets "Live Pigeons not for Liberation." (A.M. Form 1528).

Lofts are not supplied except in cases of exceptional necessity and it is only possible to obtain issues of corn on "Action Stations" or when birds are employed on a regular service.

Training of Personnel. (i) The use of Pigeons as a means of intercommunication; (ii) The Feeding and Care of Pigeons; (iii) The Handling of Pigeons.

Employment of Pigeons. Pigeons should only be used when other means of intercommunication have failed, or are not practicable, as the pigeons have to be carried to the unit using them and the conditions that make their use necessary may also prevent further supplies of birds from being sent up.

Before sending off a message by pigeon it is necessary to consider:—

The importance of the message.

The number of birds available.

The prospect of replacing the birds despatched.

Whether the message can be sent by any other means.

Normally two pigeons should be despatched, each carrying a copy of the message. The second pigeon should be released one minute after the first. Two pigeons, if available, should always be used with very important messages or when weather conditions are bad. If only a few pigeons are available and the prospect of getting others is doubtful one bird may be used, the second copy of the message being sent by some other means, or the pigeon that takes the next message.

In cases of emergency only when it is desired to send three or four messages by one pigeon a message carrier can be attached to each leg.

Pigeon Message Forms. These are made of special thin paper and are issued in pads containing forms for 8 or 16 messages in triplicate. If a sharp pencil is used a long report can be written on two forms. Writing must be clear (block capitals) as the paper becomes crumpled in the carrier. The back of the form may be used for a sketch map.

All particulars required by the form should be filled in, e.g., sender's name, time of origin, number of copies sent, etc.

Code names, if allotted to units, will invariably be used if mentioned in message.

Feeding and Care of Pigeons over Short Periods. (i) *Food.* Only the food supplied with the birds must be used. They should not be fed until they have been away from their loft for 24 hours. Thereafter 1 oz. per bird half an hour before sunset. All soiled food should be removed from the basket. Pigeons should not be fed immediately before a flight. A bird released hungry will endeavour to get to its usual feeding place (the loft) as soon as possible, whereas one which is thirsty will seek first for water. This not only delays the message but greatly increases the risk of the bird being shot or captured by the enemy, therefore—

(ii) *Water.* A continual supply of clean drinking water must be kept where the birds can find it easily. If possible, use a trough which can be attached to the outside of the basket.

(iii) *Protection from weather and mud.* Baskets should be placed or protected so that rain or mud will not splash the birds. A pigeon with wet or mud-encrusted feathers will be hampered in its flight.

(iv) *Baskets* must be kept in the fresh air as much as possible, but not in a draught. Baskets must be kept clean—also drinking troughs.

(v) *Rats.* Baskets containing pigeons must be guarded from rats.

(vi) *Disease* or sickness may be caused by the neglect of any of the above.

Handling of Pigeons. Pigeons must always be handled in the correct manner—thumb across the back, first finger under the vent and the remaining three fingers resting on the breast in front of the legs. It should then be lifted out of the basket head first; otherwise it will struggle and its wings or tail may be damaged.

Message Carriers. The message carrier at present in use is a red bakelite cylinder with a screw cap. Attached to the screw cap is a split rod. The message form is folded into a strip slightly narrower than the length of this rod, placed in the slit and twisted tightly. It is then inserted into the cylinder and the cap is partially screwed up, i.e., until the flat portion is opposite the projection on the side of the cylinder.

The message carrier is then fixed to the bakelite ring on the pigeon's leg by sliding the projecting portion *downwards* into the groove on the ring as far as it will go. The screw cap is then given a final twist. The rounded portion will then be below the groove and the carrier locked.

To remove the message reverse the above operation.

(A) STRATEGY AND TACTICS.

(1) **Strategy and Tactics.** It may be thought unnecessary for Home Guards to bother about strategy and tactics. This is not correct. They need not make a profound study of the subject but some knowledge of them enables men to "do their stuff" on guard or patrol with greater intelligence and with more probability of helping the defence as a whole.

(2) No one has ever succeeded in exactly defining where strategy ends and tactics begin. The easiest way is to take some examples:—In view of the possibility of invasion, air attack, landings by air-borne troops and parachutists, our highest military authorities have distributed the forces at their disposal in such a way as to be ready for any such attack—this is a "Strategic" distribution; when an attack comes, or several simultaneous attacks, the measures ordered by authority are "strategical"—when our forces get to grips with the enemy the action becomes "tactical," but in every case of tactics there is still a strategical aspect.

(3) Take the following very small-scale example, which is an exact reproduction of a night operation carried out by a patrol of H.G. in the very early days when we were still L.D.V.

Patrol-leader had 10 men and 1 D.R. He was informed that enemy were supposed to have landed on the coast about twenty miles away and were advancing North (*i.e.*, towards the East and West defensive line held by that particular Battalion). Enemy were reported to have motor vehicles.

His orders were to go and hold a road block, A.

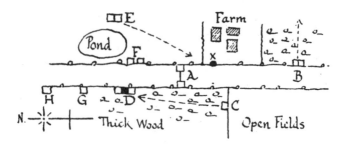

He made these dispositions:—

Two men with 30 Molotovs concealed by hedge and bank, with a little improved cover. Hedge wired and a clear line of retreat. One rifle, one shot-gun at B.

One rifleman similarly covered, with a perfect view for hundreds of yards to his front and right. He had a clear run back to Patrol-leader at D—this path being equally suitable for the Patrol-leader and his spare men to advance to the edge of the wood at C.

D is a group consisting of Patrol-leader and 2 riflemen, covering the block A. (He would have preferred the other side of the road **because that is the easier side to shoot at A from**, but at this particular place the concrete blocks get in the way).

E. Two flankers to watch that side, with orders to come in as shown (dotted) in case of attack.

F. Two riflemen bringing, with D, crossfire on A.

G and H. One rifleman and D.R. keeping a lookout northwards in case of enemy having got round or ready for friendly reinforcements or messengers. The D.R.'s car was off the road and ready to start at once in either direction.

(4) Now, would you call that a tactical distribution or a strategical? It does not much matter, the point is that I want you to think of the strategical as well as the tactical aspect of every problem. If the Patrol-leader had been content just to spread his men around in likely places (like a village eleven on the cricket field) that might be called "tactics," but just as a Captain, like Arthur Gilligan, "sets" his field with the greatest care, skill and cunning, so also did this Patrol-leader exhibit "strategy."

(5) Suppose that Patrol-leader to have had time to think out a more permanent and elaborate scheme of defence. He might argue thus "The Germans have several methods of attack (a) to come on in armoured vehicles and try to destroy posts by sheer weight; (b) to attack with highly mobile columns of infantry or cyclists who, on finding opposition, will immediately split up and infiltrate on both flanks.

"I have done the best I can for the possible attack to-night but I am going to make sure that in the event of infiltration the enemy shall not be able to mop me up from the flanks.

"By this method of infiltration he hopes to do one of two things to my particular post (a) to mop us up as he passes or (b) to force us to withdraw because we are afraid of being cut off.

"When the enemy does succeed in infiltrating **the very worst thing a post can do is to withdraw and abandon its road-block or strongpoint.**

"Therefore as soon as I can I shall construct **all-round** protection for this road-block and be prepared to hold it to the last round. I must therefore insist on being supplied with reserve food, ammunition and bombs and try to get my garrison reinforced."

(6) Now—I ask you—is it not true that there is more in the handling of one small patrol than mere drill or routine tactics? In this particular illustration the strategical aspect far outweighs the tactical in importance.

(7) Some people have a hazy idea that "strategy" and "stratagem" are the same sort of thing. They are not; stratagem comes under the Osterley Park syllabus.

(8) To resume the narrative, the Patrol on arrival mounted the five heavy rails on the road-block in under 2½ minutes, a fine example of "drill" for Home Guards in the highest sense of the word. There is drill on the parade ground which is the foundation of training to be a citizen soldier, there is drill on the road, in the fields, on the hillside and so on which, though still drill, is the basis for tactical action. It is not until your drill is applied to some definite problem that it becomes tactics. And if your tactical problem—however great or small—requires the consideration of various alternatives then it has a strategical aspect and however horrible your task do not be afraid to recognise this fact.

(B) TACTICAL EXERCISES.

(1) It is absolutely essential that all combatants, umpires, etc., be provided beforehand with three things:—

    (a)   General Idea.

    (b)   Special Idea.

    (c)   Operation Orders.

(2) **The General Idea** is what would be known in war to both sides, *e.g.*, "Enemy landings have taken place at such and such points accompanied by motor vehicles. The Home Guard may be expected to resist on successive lines of defence. Attackers will wear white helmet covers." The shorter this is the better.

(3) **The Special Idea** is a paper issued to each of the sides to tell them what they would know in war that would be unknown to the other side. Obviously, each side must have a different Special Idea.

For example: "**Special Idea** (Attack). A mobile force consisting of . . . . . . etc., has landed at . . . . . . and established a base. Columns consisting of . . . . . . are to move North as quickly as possible to try to reach . . . . . . Resistance may be expected on the lines . . . . . . and . . . . . ."

"**Special Idea** (Defence). Troops are to defend the line . . . . . . Available troops are . . . . . . Reinforcements from the North may be expected by . . . . . . a.m."

(4) Those are quite full enough—all that is wanted is for the stage to be set in a plausible way. Nothing is more worthless or heart-breaking than an exercise where nobody knows what they are doing or why.

(5) **Operation Orders** are simple or complicated according to the size of the force and the complexity of their task.

In the case just illustrated operation orders might have been as follows:—

(N.B. If urgent these might be given verbally by Section Commander to Patrols).

Operation Order No. . . . . . .   Copy No. 4

by . . . . . . Commanding . . . . . . Platoon.

1 Attack by enemy tanks is expected from the South.

2 . . . Company is to hold Road blocks A. X. V. Z.

3 . . . Platoon will hold A. and X.

4 . . . Section will hold A. with a patrol consisting of leader and not less than 10 men. Remainder of section to remain in support on Road A.

5 I shall be with the remainder of the platoon in Reserve at Cross-roads A.X.

(6) **Operation Orders** on every scale from orders for a pitched battle down to a verbal order to one man to go and do something always take the same form:—

a First you tell him what **he** ought to know.

b Next you tell him what **you** intend to do.

c Next you tell him what **he** has got to do.

In formal written Operation Orders this is the framework always to be adhered to:—

Operation Order No. . . . . . .   Copy No. . . . . . .
                    by   Date . . . . . .
. . . . Commanding . . . . Battalion.

Information 1 (a) The enemy is . . . . . . (b) Our army is . . . . . .

Intention 2. This Battalion will attack . . . . . .

Detailed Orders 3. Here give in detail what each unit or sub-division is to do as part of the General Scheme.

Where reports are to be sent 4. Battalion H.Q. will be at . . . . . . Reports to be sent to . . . . . . where Bn.-Commander will have an advanced H.Q.

Acknowledge.   Signed (by C.O. or Staff Officer).

issued by D.R.

at (time)

Copy No. 1 to . . . . . .

Copy No. 2 to . . . . . . etc.

That is all Home Guards need know about Operation Orders.

(7) Finally, about tactical exercises. These may be of immense value or pure boredom.

To be of value they must be carefully prepared by somebody with imagination. Start with something short and simple by daylight, then do simple things by night. Gradually work up to bigger schemes. Try to interest the men and induce them to "play." It is really like playing at Indians or Soldiers again and if we can persuade them that it is not childish but of real value in teaching about war they will derive great benefit; if they are not interested the best laid scheme will gang agley. I hold the view very strongly that a little realism helps—for example it is far more amusing to shoot at a figure representing Hitler than at a round black bullseye.

CHAPTER XVI.
(A) Co-operation with Military, Police and Civil Defence Services.
(B) Alarm by Church Bells. (C) Joint Action by Military, H.G. and Civil Authorities.
(D) Combined Exercises.

(A) CO-OPERATION WITH MILITARY, POLICE AND CIVIL DEFENCE SERVICES.

(1) H.G. are part of the Military Forces, at present "part-time," but on emergency possibly "whole-time." The Civil Defence services are primarily for the protection of life and property and to mitigate air-raid damage. The Police, in addition to their peace-time functions, would on emergency exercise wider powers because of their greater responsibilities. During active operations, if there is any actual attack or invasion, clearly the Armed Forces, *i.e.*, the military (including members or units of the other "fighting" services) must take supreme authority in the arena of operations.

(2) It is obvious that all these services must know and understand each other—must know what each is for, what it does and how, and must learn the methods, the drill—even the language of the others.

(3) To avoid overlapping in times of crisis and, more important still, actual obstruction of or interference with other services we must all work in together NOW so as to co-operate effectively when the time comes for action.

(4) For these reasons contact has been established between H.G. and Police. Equally cordial contact must be made with A.R.P. organisations and—whenever there are military in the neighbourhood—with the soldiers also.

(5) This is not merely a kind of pious resolution that the higher authorities in the different services shall work together when the day comes, it is a definite duty of every member of the H.G. to know personally as many as possible of the other Services in his home locality and to swap information. If we do this now we shall avoid the inconvenience and danger of holding up the work of others, especially by night.

(6) We should all know by what uniforms, badges or identity cards

properly authorised persons can be recognised and it should be a point of honour **never**, from a stupid belief in red-tape, to obstruct a genuine member of another Service and never, through slackness, to let a suspicious character pass.

(7) It is pretty difficult but we are all up against difficulties and they are only created to be surmounted.

(B) ALARM BY CHURCH BELLS.

(1) Church bells will only be rung to give the alarm in case of authenticated landings from the air of enemy troops.

(2) The authority for ringing bells is the military or H.G. Commander on the spot.

(3) Church bells in neighbouring towns and villages will not take up the alarm unless there are actually invaders also in that locality.

(4) Bells must only be rung on the most certain and accurate information, consequently Commanders of H.G. units in whose area there is a Church with bells must prepare and plan NOW to ensure that on receipt of such definite information:

(a) A responsible man who can ring the bells is ready for instant action at every Church.

(b) Such man shall not be interfered with by neighbouring units or Civil Services.

(C) JOINT ACTION BY MILITARY, H.G. AND CIVIL AUTHORITIES

In the event of invasion of any part of the country a workable scheme for co-ordinating the several functions of military and civil authorities must be ready for operation in that locality on principles laid down by the highest authority.

Close liaison exists between Army Commanders and Regional Commissioners and the Police are represented at Corps Headquarters, and conferences are continually being held on this level between Military and Civil. On the larger scale plans have been made and co-ordinated for the higher direction of civil and military concerns together, and on a smaller scale similar local schemes have been or are to be worked out.

In the Military lay-out, the C.-in-C. commands armies consisting of Army Corps and Army troops. Each Corps consists of Divisions and

Corps troops. Each Division consists of Brigades and Divisional troops. The Brigade is a compact formation of all arms in which are fighting units, Battalions, Regiments, and so on, and services such as engineers, medical personnel, etc.

Some formations occupy an area for the defence of which they are responsible, others are kept concentrated and mobile with the intention of moving them with great rapidity to any point dictated by strategy or tactics. Obviously such a mobile force, though it may have collaborated in a scheme, cannot be expected to operate it if the force is sent post-haste into a different part of the country.

It is for the defence forces with a more sedentary role to co-operate with Local Authorities in the scheme of local administration.

Let us now examine the lay-out of "Local Authorities."

The essential feature of the "chain of command" in the Army is the invariable principle that the Commander really does command all formations under him, and so on down the ladder to the lowest rung. In Local Government this principle does not apply. You would suppose that in a system consisting of Ministry, County Councils, Borough and other Councils, and Parishes, there would be the same sort of chain of command, but this is not so. The lay-out looks like the military lay-out, but the machine functions differently. It is not suggested that there is anything wrong with this, but it is necessary to examine the facts rather than to take two rather similar diagrams and think they are the same. The Rural District Council consists of the members of the council and their officers and staff, *e.g.* Clerk, Building Surveyor, Sanitary Inspector, Medical Officer of Health, etc. They have wide powers in their district, and are not definitely under the orders of the County Council as a Brigade is under the orders of a Division, though the County Council have a great deal to say about the administration and carry out certain functions in which District has no say, *e.g.* police, schools, roads and other matters. A fair idea of the County Council's powers of this kind may be got from the items which are lumped together as the County contribution on the rate demand note.

Similarly, Parish Councils are not directly under the orders of the District Council. They have very small powers, and very often do not exercise such powers as they have, but all serving on them, as on District Councils, must be regarded by the military as very valuable collaborators.

It must be emphasised here that on the administrative map of England the jig-saw I am describing is even more complex. Not only do the boundaries of Local Authorities tend to spill over, but they do not necessarily coincide with other "districts," such as Postal and Police, nor, for example, with the Grid System. How much more is it likely to be complicated by superimposing military formations (not permanent) whose distribution is not governed at all by local administrative routine, but by tactical requirements and available billeting accommodation?

The District Council has many other attachments particularly in war-time, *e.g.* with offices under various Ministries, such as Civil Defence, Food, Fuel and the like, and in order to carry out its duties—so much heavier than in peace time—it has to employ extra personnel, and every member of the staff has to fill at least two roles. Thus you may find the Sanitary Inspector also Chief A.R.P. Officer, and when the time comes to operate a joint military and civil scheme you may well find him functioning eventually under the military Commander.

The H.G. has a lay-out with something in common with the military and something with the civil. It is partly territorial and partly based on a military organisation, by units.

The country is divided into "Zones," usually corresponding with County Council areas. If the zone is large it is divided into "Groups," each group consisting of a convenient number (about four as a rule) of battalions.

Each Battalion is divided into companies, platoons and sections without any fixed "establishment" as in the army, in fact the strength of any unit depends on local conditions and numbers available.

The Battalion and Company are administrative units, but as a general rule the Platoon is likely to be the tactical unit except in urban areas where a company may be so concentrated as to be capable of being commanded in action by an officer senior to a platoon commander.

The H.G. are enrolled with the essential duty of defending their own homes and are not normally required to go more than a mile or two from where they live; in rural areas platoons are scattered all over the place, whereas in towns we may find companies and even battalions concentrated in a locality the size of a platoon area in the country.

Look at the map of a specific Rural District. The H.G. organisation does not exactly coincide with this, but it corresponds to it. At least it can be said that companies and platoons are closely associated with definite administrative areas.

The local Regular Commander is responsible for the operational command of Regulars and H.G. in his area and prepares a defence scheme under the orders of his superior Commander. When this defence scheme is complete from the strategical and tactical points of view the higher authorities, Military and Civil (*e.g.* Corps Commanders and Regional Commissioner), agree upon a joint plan, and each of them sends down through his own channels instructions to the local Commanders and Authorities as to how the local scheme is to be elaborated. The local Commanders and Authorities are presumably already in close touch, and on receipt of orders from above can put the final touches to a scheme for local operation.

Co-ordination of specialised services such as A.R.P. and the military would be settled in detail by conferences called by the Government Department concerned. Some of the problems to be covered in advance if confusion is to be avoided on the approach of the enemy to any locality are these:—

Medical Services and Hospitals, epidemics, sanitation, food and fuel, water and petrol.

Transportation, Roads, Railways, Bridges.

Utility Services, Communications.

Control of Civilians, Evacuation, Traffic Control.

A.R.P., Fire Services, etc.

It may be accepted that in all defended localities and nodal points there is now a Military Commander and a "Civil Representative," and that between them there is a clear understanding how their respective duties dovetail and overlap and at what stage responsibility may be shifted from one to the other.

The Home Guard may, therefore, rest assured that their interests not only as soldiers, but as citizens with families and dependants in the immediate neighbourhood of the place where they themselves may be called upon to fight, are being looked after with all the thoroughness of which the higher authorities are capable. If a Home Guard Company or Platoon Commander is not satisfied that all is well he should consult his operational Commander, the Local Authority and the Police.

(D) COMBINED EXERCISES.

(1) Certain places are described as nodal points, others are defended localities with the same machinery, i.e., Triumvirate with or without garrison. The same principles should apply to all of them in action, and in exercises designed to test their efficient working.

(2) The machinery is a Triumvirate of (*a*) Military Commander (or Deputy); (*b*) Civil Representative and (*c*) Police. These should already be a working committee who meet and consider all problems that may arise in invasion, or blitz, or sporadic attack, or when enemy action may disturb normal life, e.g., by a bomb, or fire or crashed plane.

This Triumvirate should have, working with them and in agreement, all the civil services such as fire, casualties, medical arrangements, control of the inhabitants, sanitary services, food, water and so on, and in a well-run locality these services are dealt with by sub-committees, and the whole locality is in fact organized to meet any eventuality.

(3) A clear distinction must be drawn between the routine of a Triumvirate and an *exercise* designed to test their efficiency.

If the organization has been well thought out the action of the Triumvirate is routine and will stand or fall by the work they have put in to adapt local government conditions to emergency needs.

But *exercises* to test their efficiency are on an entirely different footing. For an exercise to have any practical value it must be run on the lines which military experience has proved to be indispensable for instructional purposes.

(4) A number of recent exercises prove that unless the whole scheme has been thought out and clearly defined by some guiding authority, the result is chaos in execution and little to be learnt from the subsequent inquest.

It is essential to define the relative responsibilities of the Triumvirate.

I have submitted this view recently to higher authority, and it has not yet been contradicted. I think it is the only practical basis:

When fighting takes place or is imminent the Military Commander will assume control. The Military Commander is the sole judge of when that situation arises. There is no magic formula which shall invest the Military Commander with the executive authority which, in the absence of specific orders from higher authority, he will exercise absolutely at his own discretion.

(5) If that is a correct interpretation I can deal with test exercises.

(6) For a joint exercise between military and civil services, these are the essentials:

(*a*) A Director (and Chief Umpire) who will set the scheme on paper as a military exercise is set;

(*b*) The scheme should be primarily to test the working of the Triumvirate, their reaction to sudden and unexpected situations, and the response of the civil services to their orders.

The introduction of fighting by Regulars or H.G. should be incidental so as to present a new situation, but never so as to make the battle the chief item on the programme.

After all, the troops can fight battles at any time but the Civil Defences can only profit if the scheme is set primarily for them;

(*c*) The Director (and Chief Umpire) should issue (on paper):—(e.g.) General idea: "Landings from the air are expected."

Special idea: "(Triumvirate) Be prepared to Stand To or go to Action Stations at short notice."

Special Idea: "(Attacking Force) Be prepared to simulate a landing of Paratroops at . . . with the object of . . . and . . ."

The special ideas are secret and should be kept as simple as possible. Ambitious schemes defeat their purpose;

(*d*) The Director should meet and discuss with his assistant umpires (military, police and civil) all the points on which he proposes to test the Triumvirate and their organization *before the operation*, so that they all know what the game is;

(*e*) Every test and incident and accident should be laid down beforehand with time and place defined and it should *be on paper* to make the subsequent inquest easier;

(*f*) The military member of the Triumvirate *must* be in command throughout the exercise. He must be deemed to have exercised his authority to take over control as though it were a real enemy attack. He must be in a position to say that the civil authorities and the troops are to remain at "Stand To" or "Action Stations" or to stand down at his discretion. If he has not that authority the different services will dribble away because it is raining or because they are tired of inaction and the troops will very likely go on with their battle which was only intended to be a back ground to action by the Civil Defence Services.

(7) There need not be H.G. or Troops in every scheme and if they *are* included they may be token forces.

(8) Incidents should be worked in in such a way as to necessitate the Triumvirate *all* doing something, e.g., sudden arrival of refugees; here is a case for police and welfare workers and also H.G. action in case there are boches among the refugees. Or again, crash-landing of an unidentified plane—here is work for every department.

(9) All participating should keep a war diary, however brief, showing times of incidents, messages sent and received and action taken.

(10) Visitors seeking instruction should be welcome, but visitors at the same time from the different ladders in the chain of command are to be deprecated. Suppose, for example, an exercise is set and run by a Battalion Commander. He would welcome the presence of (say) one Zone, Group, Division or Brigade Commander, but their combined presence has the tendency to turn a simple exercise into a formal inspection. Even with the best intentions they are apt to be regarded as too many cooks.

(11) On conclusion of the exercise there must be an immediate pow-wow attended by all umpires and heads of the different services, presided over by the Director (and Chief Umpire). Otherwise no lessons will be learnt. Nobody will bother to read a summing-up on paper of a battle in which each thinks he has won.

(12) Finally, the scheme should be simple and snappy, to be got over in the prescribed time and no aftermath. And another scheme, and another and another, should be carried out without warning.

(A) OFFICE WORK.

(1) The first principle is that only what is really necessary to improve the efficiency of the H.G. should ever be written or published or read.

There are certain Forms and Returns which must be completed to give Higher Authority a picture of what really exists. There are many subjects which require that the Battalion Commander or Staff or the Company Commander shall write a letter or an answer, but correspondence must be reduced to its lowest terms and to a minimum.

There are certain things to avoid. The first is the tendency to write for the sake of writing. The second is "jargon." The third is the desire to put on paper what can be done by word of mouth.

"Jargon" obscures all aspects of office work, it is like the smoke-screen of the cuttle fish.

"This Pro forma should be signed at the base of the reverse of the Form and not at the foot of the face"—this is an authentic last-war record. It means "Sign over-page."

Why "Pro forma" or the horrible plural "Pro formæ"? There is a technical differentiation between "State," "Return," "Proforma," "Specimen Form" and "Form," but for the H.G. the simple English word "Form" is enough. There are certain forms that *must* be filled in—for example, Army Form B2599.

If anybody sends you jargon tear it up and put it in the paper salvage bag. There is no single subject of interest to H.G. that cannot be put into plain English.

There are only three reasons for not being clear: (i) the writer does not know what he means to say; (ii) he does not know how to say it; (iii) he knows all right but does not want to say it. All of these are criminal in anybody who thinks he can run a H.G. organisation or Battalion or Platoon, just because he has got a clerk, a typewriter and a Roneo.

(2) *Correspondence. Signing of Papers.*

Home Guard correspondence should follow Army rules.

(*a*) ALL correspondence to a higher formation must be signed by or "for" the Commander of the Battalion, and not by his staff on their own behalf.

(*b*) Correspondence on policy and principle should be signed by the Commander personally. In specially urgent cases it is legitimate to sign "for" a Commander, but it should be indicated that he has approved the draft, though not available to sign.

(*c*) Similarly correspondence from Companies should be addressed Battalion H.Q. and signed by or "for" the Commanding Officer. Correspondence from Battalion to Companies is signed by Adjutant or Staff Officer. This does not prevent Battalion Commander and Officer Commanding Company addressing each other direct when appropriate, but usually the above procedure is correct and saves time.

(*d*) It follows from (*a*) above that Medical and other technical officers must only correspond with higher formations through the Commanding Officer. The medical arrangements of a Battalion are the concern of the Commanding Officer; the Medical Officer is his adviser. The Medical Officer may answer technical letters that come down through medical and not Staff channels, and if he does write he should do so to the H.G. Medical Adviser, and NOT to the Regular A.D.M.S.

(3) *Correspondence.* Use of Army Form C.2128.

There are far too many subjects dealt with by memos and telephone conversations.

Each memo requires drafting and typing with heading, address, etc., and most of the telephone conversations involve a lot of busy people in making personal contact between two of them who ought to be busy also, and the result is often delay and waste of time by conversation drifting into irrelevant channels.

The Message Form is a very old friend that has fallen into neglect. In fact many use it as a scribbling pad and do not know how to fill it in properly. Every Commanding Officer, Staff Officer and Clerk should have a pad of C. 2128 and carbon paper at his elbow. Before drafting any memo or making a call, he should consider—"Can I do this by Message Form?" The answer is usually "Yes." He then writes:—

(i) (TO) C. Coy.

    (FROM) Adjt.   P.33   23.2.42.   BJ60

        Report number of unused sandbags in possession.

            (Signed) P. Wicklefidget, Q.M. for Adjt.

or (ii) (TO) GROUP. Repeated Bde.

    (FROM) 64 Sussex H.G   OK43.   23.2.42.   B.F.164

        Exercise arranged for A. Coy. commencing 1900 hrs.

            (Signed) A. Clatterbox, Adjt. for C.O.

The Despatch Clerk puts message (i) in an envelope and posts it, and files the carbon copy.

The Telephone Operator takes first opportunity of telephoning (ii), marks the message "despatched 1130 hrs.," and hands it in due course to the office for filing.

The form is the result of years of experience, and I seriously commend its use to all H.G. who wish to help in reducing clerical labour, waste of time and paper.

It will be found a simple matter for the officer concerned to number his messages serially from day to day, but the appropriate file reference number should be entered under "Originator's Number" before despatch.

(4) *Bumph* . . . My son, be admonished; of making many books there is no end; and much bumph is a weariness of the flesh.

Periodically there are pious resolutions to reduce paper work and every resolution results in an increase. The H.G. who are supposed to be outside the official paper chase are in fact swamped and stifled by the volume of output, much of which is useless and much of which fails in its intention because there is so much to read and digest that it goes unread and undigested.

I know that this curse can be controlled because I have done it on every scale from Command to Army Corps, Division, Garrison and Unit (it must be noted that I am only referring to instructions, orders and circulars of general application and not to direct correspondence between formation and unit).

Some of the fundamental principles are these:

(*a*) Nothing should ever be published if it is not worth publication.

(*b*) If worth publication, it should be sub-edited and reduced to its lowest terms by a harmless drudge who is only concerned with the problem of putting into clear, concise and complete English, the gist of the original draft.

(*c*) A printing press with standard type and size of paper at H.Q. saves

This message may be sent AS WRITTEN by any means)	(If liable to be intercepted or fall into enemy hands, this message must be sent in cipher.)	(Originator's Instructions, Degree of Priority.) POST

many duplicating machines, clerks and copying errors in lower formations. Enough copies should be printed to reach everybody concerned.

(*d*) If a lower formation has anything of wider interest, it should be

(This message may be sent AS WRITTEN by any means.)	(If liable to be intercepted, or fall into enemy hands, this message must be sent in cipher.)	(Originator's Instructions. Degree of Priority.) TELEPHONE Immediate.

sent to higher formation for dissemination from there, in print.

(*e*) In lower formations the old message form A.F.C.2128 should be used whenever possible to cut out the pernicious habit of wasting the time of many people by long telephone talks and the deplorable waste of time and paper in dictating and typing with full headlines memoranda which can be dealt with by message form.

(*f*) In the H.G. practically all the Platoon Commander's correspondence should be confined to what he gets from above and replies in message form from himself. It is true he must keep his record of attendance and claims for subsistence, but all the rest of it should be done at Company or Battalion H.Q. level.

(B) NOTES ON ENROLMENT.
AGRICULTURAL, CIVIL DEFENCE AND INDUSTRIAL WORKERS AND HOME GUARD

The following notes explain to agricultural and industrial workers the conditions under which they would be trained, equipped and armed, and employed on "Action Stations" if they enrolled in the H.G.

The ideal is for every able-bodied man to be able to fight and kill boches in emergency—however exacting or important his normal work may be. We cannot kill boches satisfactorily without weapons, training, discipline and organisation—these the H.G. can supply. Determination, self-sacrifice and guts are equally necessary. These must be contributed by the man himself and there is no doubt that the voluntary acceptance of such service will not only make him a better fighting man but also a better man.

The following remarks apply equally to men in Civil Defence Services and in industrial concerns and other businesses of national importance particularly agriculture, and I hope they may clear the air.

Men are divided into two categories (List (i) and List (ii)). The former are what might be called full-time H.G. and will be mustered immediately on "Action Stations." The men in List (ii) are those whose primary duty is some work of national importance which prevents their being full-time H.G.'s either now or on "Action Stations." They are also not necessarily mustered immediately on "Action Stations" but only for such time and such periods as their civil superior can release them for duty. Most men in A.R.P. services and many in agriculture and industrial works who enrol in the H.G. will be on List (ii).

They will be clothed, equipped, armed and trained just like any other H.G. They will not, however, be made to do H.G. duty or service that would interfere with their primary duty of keeping their work going.

For all Civil Defence, agricultural workers and utility men, duties are in this order of importance:—

(1) Their civil job.

(2) Their H.G. training and routine duties.

(3) Fighting on "Action Stations" or as soon after as their civil superior can release them.

It is obvious that once a man is trained and qualified to take his place in the ranks, his Commanding Officer can release him from guard and routine duties if they would add unduly to his hours of work. It would be for such men to keep touch with their Platoon by conscientiously attending parade when they can.

The following are, roughly, the conditions of service in the H.G. whether a volunteer or directed by the Ministry of Labour:—

(1) The man must be enrolled in an existing Company without regard to whether a special unit is to be formed in his works. He then becomes

a H.G. with all his rights and duties.

(2) He must be trained. *His Commanding Officer cannot require of him more than 48 hours in a period of four weeks*, including picquet and routine duties. He may do as much more as he pleases.

(3) When trained his Commanding Officer will consider his individual case and may release him from such duties as conflict with his civil occupation.

(4) When on duty or training he is entitled to subsistence allowance for continuous periods of duty at the rate of 1s. 6d. for a period not less than 5 hours or 3s. not less than 8 hours.

(5) When "mustered" on "Stand To" a H.G. becomes entitled to compensation for loss of wages at the rate of 12s. a day, up to 70s. a week, less deductions for rations and insurance. When "mustered" on "Action Stations" all H.G. are entitled to compensation at 7s. a day (with a later right to appeal for a higher rate up to 12s.) without deductions.

(6) When enrolled in the H.G. he becomes a soldier with considerable latitude of "give and take"; on being "mustered," which means that the crisis of invasion is upon us, he becomes as much a soldier as any other soldier in the Service. But if he is in Civil Defence or utility works or on important agricultural work he will not be ordered away from his civil job until his own boss can let him go.

That is the whole story in few words. A man who joins the H.G. will be ready to kill boches with a clean weapon and a clear conscience, and methodically like a member of a team instead of one of a rabble. Remember that however tough the individuals may be a rabble can never fight like an army.

(C) COMPENSATION FOR LOSS OF EARNINGS.

(1) On "Stand to," all key men mustered, whether for manning road blocks or other duties will, if they are losing wages, be paid at the rate of 12s. a day up to a maximum of £3 10s. per week, less appropriate deductions for insurance and food, under A.C.I.1272 of 1941, para. 1 (a).

(2) On "Action Stations" following "Stand To," the simplified procedure laid down in para. 4 of A.C.I.1272/41 as amended by A.C.I.2021/41 will be adopted for all men entitled to compensation, including those already mustered. This payment will be at the rate of 7s. a day, and no deduction will be made for feeding. In this connection it is

pointed out that where the simplified arrangements apply it will subsequently be open to members to claim any balance of actual loss up to 12s. a day, subject to appropriate deductions.

(3) A sum which is estimated to meet the requirements of the Battalion to cover payments for rations during the first fortnight and payments for compensation for loss of earnings in respect of the first week has been lodged with the bank. Payment will be made on presentation at the bank of a letter from the Commanding Officer of the Battalion stating that the Unit has been called out for service and requesting that the initial amount may be placed to its credit forthwith, so that cash can be drawn immediately.

Further funds required after the initial period will be obtained by the Commanding Officer from the Territorial Army Association on weekly requisition. If normal banking procedure is suspended, funds will be supplied to Battalion Commanders by mobile cashiers.

(D) PROFICIENCY BADGE TESTS.

After careful study by a representative committee in a H.G. Zone, the following memorandum was drawn up and widely followed. It is offered as a guide to something better.

MEMORANDUM.

(Conditions are laid down in A.C.I.491 of 1941, and Home Guard Instruction No. 14 of 1940 which must be adhered to, but as there is some difference of opinion as to the correct interpretation of the Instructions, the following outline may help Battalion Commanders who are, of course, at liberty to adopt whatever other procedure they prefer within the terms of the War Office Instruction.)

(1) A.C.I.491 of 1941 and H.G. instruction No. 14 of 1940.

This badge must be regarded as an honourable sign of real H.G. proficiency and not as a thing that anybody can get for the asking. The standard should be kept very high and tests should as far as possible be uniform throughout the Zone. No man should be tested until his Company Commander considers that he is (*a*) a first-class all-round H.G., and (*b*) qualified to pass the very limited prescribed tests with distinction. Men must be tested by impartial examiners, i.e., by expert officers from other Companies, or by Regular Officers from affiliated Battalions, etc., or assisted by them. Battalion Commanders should keep Regular Operational Commanders informed of tests to be carried out, to give an opportunity of supervision when convenient.

(2) The tests actually laid down are:—

(*a*) *General Knowledge.* To answer correctly four questions out of five on subjects such as local knowledge of post offices, railway and police stations, roads to and from neighbouring villages and towns, and topography generally. Local organisation of H.G. units, their H.Q., Commanding Officers, war stations, etc., and the same, in general terms, regarding Regular Troops and local defence services. This general knowledge test could be made easy enough for a child or difficult enough to stump a Commanding Officer. What is wanted is a searching examination to see that the candidate has an intelligent knowledge of the locality.

(*b*) *Rifle Efficiency.* Aiming, trigger-pressing, snap-shooting, rapid-firing, shooting with .22 on miniature range, and open range. The details are given in H.G. Instruction No. 14, Appendix A, Para. 2, but it is not clear when the candidate is supposed actually to load with dummy or to operate the bolt. War Office has ruled: Dummies should always be used, and it is ruled that H.G. Instruction, No. 14, Appendix A (2) implies the use of dummies where they are available. The following are suitable rules for Home Guard:—

(i) No eye-disc will ever be used with dummy; in fact, H.G. need never use an eye-disc at all.

(ii) Except in "fixed aiming" from a rest, all tests of trigger-pressing, snap-shooting, and rapid-firing will be done with dummy. The examiners will pay particular attention to the efficiency in loading and unloading which is as important as accuracy of aim. They may use aim-correcter, or mirror, or any method they wish.

(iii) The standard on miniature range has now been lowered (H.G. Instruction No. 33) to a 2-inch group at 25 yards. The candidate will be required to fire off his test at a given time and place, and not be passed on some particular group he has made at practice. He should (at the discretion of the examiners) be given not more than three tries of five rounds each, and he will only be given a second and third try if his first group shows signs of marksmanship. War Office has ruled: The number of times a man can shoot to pass his test must be governed by the Commanding Officer's discretion.

(iv) The test on open range should be to get 5 shots on to an 8-in. bull at 100 yards. Not more than two attempts to be allowed. Home Guard Instruction No. 14 certainly says: "grouping rather than application to be practised. 8-in. group at 100 yards," but "practising" must not be confused with test, and a H.G. is not fit for a Proficiency Badge unless he can group 5 shots on an 8-in. bull at 100 yards with a service rifle of whichever type is available.

(v) The remaining test is one alternative. War Office has ruled that it is the choice of the Company Commander and not of the man which subject the candidate takes; out of four subjects—automatic weapon, field works, map-reading, or (in the case of a man who has been employed as an instructor) ability to instruct. It is not sufficient that a candidate can just scrape through on one of these. The examiners should *before submitting the man to the prescribed test* examine him generally as to his all-round proficiency, taking into consideration how he is employed in his unit. They should study his general smartness, turn-out and character, and find out from him what experience he has of such subjects as grenades, explosives, anti-tank measures, camouflage, fieldcraft, gas, first aid, etc., according to the role that is expected of him in the Home Guard. A man is not required to know all the subjects, but the examiners must prefer a good rifleman who can use live grenades, dig, wire, read a map and take charge of a patrol, or a man of similarly varied knowledge, to one who can just scrape through on the minimum tests, but whose general knowledge is deficient.

(3) This badge is a sign that the wearer is considered a proficient Home Guard by a qualified board of examiners: the tests will therefore be the same for all Home Guards, regardless of rank.

(4) Since this was first published, signalling has been added as an alternative subject and some units have adopted simple first-aid as compulsory.

(E) HOME GUARD MEDICAL ORGANISATION WITH THE PLATOON.
(With acknowledgements to the Sussex Zone Medical Adviser and Staff.)

(1) *Introductory*. These notes are intended for easy reference and are based on A.C.I.780 and para. 2 of Home Guard Information Circular No. 11, the full text of which should be studied in any case of doubt. All

reference to Regimental Aid Posts has been omitted, since no R.A.P.'s have been authorised in the Sussex Zone.

Abbreviations used (unofficial):—

C.D.—for Civil Defence and C.D. Casualty Organisation.

H.G.C.C.P.—for Home Guard casualty collecting post.

(2) *General Rules:*—

(*a*) USE CIVIL DEFENCE CASUALTY ORGANISATION WHENEVER POSSIBLE.

(*b*) The Company Commander and the Sub-Unit Medical Officer (if appointed) must keep close liaison with the local A.R.P. sub-controller, wardens and Medical Officer of Health.

(3) *Responsibility* of the H.G. for the care of its casualties is limited to:—

(*a*) Immediate first-aid treatment by the first field dressing or other available appliances, and their care until they reach C.D. Casualty Organisation, who then become responsible.

(*b*) Conveyance (by stretcher if necessary) to the Home Guard casualty collecting post.

(4) *Collection* of casualties by the H.G. will be to H.G. casualty collecting posts, to await collection by the C.D. (or Military). If there is a suitably located C.D. first-aid point it will naturally be used as the H.G.C.C.P.

(5) *Home-Guard casualty collecting posts* will normally be on a platoon basis, and within half a mile of the defended locality to keep hand carriage to a minimum. They will be in charge of the platoon medical orderly corporal. The following sequence will be observed in establishing H.G.C.C.P.'s:—

(*a*) Select position with regard to tactical plan.

(*b*) Study C.D. first-aid scheme. Use any C.D. first-aid points or posts which meet H.G. requirements. Platoon medical orderly corporal will be attached as H.G. representative. Remember that H.G. can apply for the "upgrading" of any C.D. first-aid points.

(*c*) If a H.G.C.C.P. is required where no C.D. point or post is available, C.D. should be asked to set one up. If this cannot be done, the H.G.C.C.P. will be established (if possible) in a suitable dwelling, and a joint appeal may be made to the War Organisation of the Red Cross and St. John or to the W.V.S. to help with staffing and equipment.

By this method there should be no overlapping of first-aid services and surplus posts will not be established. As casualties may require to be held for some hours, arrangements should be made for their comfort. The provision of tea, sugar and tinned milk is under consideration. Alternative positions should be planned to meet attack from any unexpected quarter.

(6) *Evacuation from H.G. casualty collecting points* will normally be by ambulance transport of C.D. to C.D. first-aid posts or E.M.S. Hospitals. Where this cannot be made available local H.G. arrangements must be made.

(7) *Medical Officers.* Battalion and Sub-Units M.G.'s are medical advisers to their respective commanders. They cannot be monitored but during operations will render such service as their civil duties permit.

(8) *Medical Orderly (Corporal).* One will be trained for each platoon. He will be responsible for the platoon first-aid equipment and in charge of the Home Guard casualty collecting post.

(9) *Stretcher-bearers* will be trained on a basis of eight per 100 men. They should be trained in the use of weapons and be regarded as a pool on which to draw for medical duties when required.

(10) *Equipment and stores* for approximately 100 men.
Basic Scale:—

Haversacks, shell dressings, filled 1
Outfits, first-aid, general, large 1
Splints, common, scored wood (set of 16) ....(set) 1
Armlets, Geneva Cross, 1 for each Medical Officer, Armlets, S.B.8
Stretchers, ambulance 2
Slings, stretchers, ambulance (1 per stretcher) 2
Blankets (for stretchers, ambulance) (3 per stretcher) 6
Bottles, water (Ordnance pattern) (1 per stretcher) 2
Carriers, W.B. (1 per stretcher) 2

For isolated sections, if required:—
Shell dressings, Standard B.P.C. dressings, triangular bandages, Tannic acid jelly.

For practice purposes:—
Bandages, loose woven, open wool, bleached, 3 ins. by 4 yds. .12
Bandages, triangular, unbleached 6

(When platoons are larger than 150 they may draw the equipment of two platoons.)

The equipment will be distributed to sub-units as advised by the Battalion Medical Officer, and all items will be kept under lock and key until active operations begin.

(11) *Isolated Sections.* Where sections are widely dispersed special application can be made for extra medical equipment (see para. 10 above) and morphia to be given under the tongue. By "isolation" is meant isolation from a doctor.

(12) *First-aid instruction.* All ranks should receive instruction in the use of the first field dressing, and in essential ?? and hygiene.

(F) HASTY DEMOLITIONS WITH EXPLOSIVES.

(Supplied by Major K. M. Hawker, 4 Sussex H.G.)

(1) Home Guards should rarely be called upon to use explosives for demolition except under the supervision of an R.E. or other expert officer, but it is possible that in certain circumstances we might be called upon to assist in placing explosives.

(2) The three explosives most likely to be used are gunpowder, guncotton and dynamite, and I will give you some idea of their effect on the object to be demolished and how the charges are placed.

(3) Gunpowder will explode by the direct application of fire, that is to say, by the use of fusee either lighted by hand or by electrical current.

Guncotton requires the use of a detonator containing a high explosive such as fulminate of mercury.

Dynamite is similar but the high explosive contained in the ordinary commercial cap is sufficient for the purpose.

(4) The fuses in use are instantaneous, safety or slow burning, and instantaneous electrical.

The instantaneous fuse is orange in colour and can be readily recognised even in the dark by its snaky covering of fine wire.

The safety use is black and burns slowly (about 3ft. per minute).

(5) In making up a charge, therefore, care must be taken to use sufficient safety fuse to allow time to get under cover before the explosion occurs.

Instantaneous fuse will have direct contact with the gunpowder or detonator and be carefully attached to the required length of safety fuse, which should be lighted by means of a fusee.

(6)

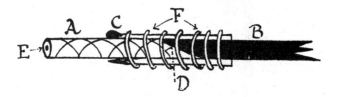

Joining fuses—A, Instantaneous fuse.
B, Safety fuse.
C, Splints formed of matches tightly bound.
D, Complete contact of fuses.
E, Quick match.
F, Binding.

(7) Gunpowder as a shaking, shattering and blasting action, guncotton a local cutting effect and dynamite is generally used for blasting.

The amount of the charge to be used in each case can be calculated usually by formulae, the details of which could only be dealt with in a more exhaustive study of the subject. The charges are exploded as follows:—

(a) Gunpowder is very suitable for quickly demolishing buildings and isolated walls or sheds.

For the hasty demolition of a house the charge should be placed inside, divided into four parts, and placed in the four corners of the building on the ground floor, and "tamped" as much as possible. All doors and windows to be tightly closed.

It is of the utmost importance that all explosives should be "tamped" so that the greatest effect may be attained.

In the case of gunpowder it can be well covered with earth and if possible some heavy article placed on top.

It is also absolutely necessary that a charge when divided up must be exploded simultaneously: to ensure this the following method is recommended:—

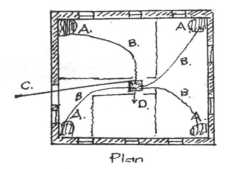

Plan

A—Charge of Gunpowder.

B—Instantaneous fuse.

C—Safety fuse, or combination of safety and instantaneous.

D—A pan or flat box containing loose gunpowder.

By this means, the Safety fuse "C," after lighting, reaches the powder in box "D" which starts the instantaneous fuse "B," thus reaching the charges "A" simultaneously.

(b) Guncotton is carried in convenient sized slabs, usually kept damp when it can be handled with safety and even cut with a saw or knife if required. Damp guncotton will not explode without the direct contact with dry guncotton. Each slab of guncotton is holed to receive a small piece of dry guncotton called a primer—the primer being also holed to receive a detonator.

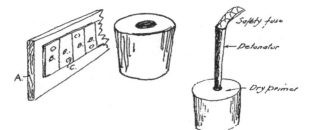

A—Board.

B—Slabs of guncotton.

C—Primer hole in each.

The amount of charge and consequently the number of slabs are ascertained by calculation.

A good method is to fasten the slabs to a board by wiring and place the full charge with the guncotton facing the object to be cut, the board being securely fastened to the object.

It is absolutely imperative that the slabs are in close contact. It is only necessary to fit up **one** primer and detonator for the series.

One-third of a slab of guncotton will cut a railway line entirely in two parts and turn up the ends of the fracture—applied and securely bound.

In attacking a steel bridge or similar erection, it is necessary to calculate the amount required to cut each member. Apply separate charges as required and explode the whole simultaneously.

A brick or stone bridge can be demolished as sketch:—

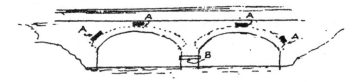

A—Charge of gunpowder placed, if possible, in close contact to the upper side of masonry arch.

B—Charges of guncotton to each pier, all exploded simultaneously.

A steel bridge can be cut by applying charges of guncotton to the vital supporting members.

Although rather expensive a tree of any size can be quickly cut through by means of a necklace of guncotton primers—these should be strung on a stout wire with close contact and one primer fixed with detonator and fuse tied to the necklace. The tree will be cut through at the point of contact.

(c) Dynamite is dangerous stuff to handle, especially in hot weather, when it is liable to become very plastic. It is particularly useful for filling up irregular surfaces and prepared holes in rocks, etc., in fact anywhere where a blasting effect is required. As previously stated, it can be exploded by the use of a commercial cap and fuse.

* * *

CAUTION:—

No explosives may be improvised or bought by H.G.

CHAPTER XVIII.
ENVOI.

This little book addressed to my comrade volunteers came rather late in the day, but having failed to get short, comprehensive official instructions I wrote it very hurriedly to fill the gap, and in preparing this revised edition I have followed the advice of authorities whom I respect, to unsay nothing and to add little.

After all, the Home Guard (or L.D.V.) were formed in a hurry and we have had, fortunately, some breathing space.

A condemned man, expecting to be taken to the scaffold, was awakened by a warder who said, "Good news for you—they have given you an hour of grace"; and the prisoner said, "O.K., show her in."

My object has been to help you to take advantage of our further hour of grace.

War—and particularly this war—is a beastly, bloody business and we may regard it from different points of view.

One day a party of brutal and licentious soldiers (like you and me) knocked at a farm-house door and a buxom wench came out and said, "Whatever you do to me, spare—oh spare—my aged grandmother." And an old crone looked out of an upper window and said, "Speak for yourself, my girl—War is war."

We are all in it, old and young, men, women and children, and I say to the H.G. and to all those people with whom their duties are interwoven, "Stick it out, good luck, good hunting and—God be with you."

* * *

I have nothing to add to the above which has appeared in the last four impressions, but I would like to close by reprinting the following from the final chapter of the September, 1940, issue:—

"What is the H.G. likely to be wanted for, over and above its present limited role?"

The answer is obvious; the Regular Army and all its reserve and reinforcement strength will be wanted for the offensive war against and into Germany and elsewhere. The Home Guard will of necessity have to take over almost entirely the land defence of the realm.

You may say that is ridiculous. The H.G. are only under an obligation to act defensively within a mile or two of their own homes, moreover, they are not soldiers in the sense that they can be *ordered* to do this or to go there.

Believe me, the Home Guard is beginning to find itself—as they say of a ship that has successfully surmounted her first difficulties—and very soon the H.G. will realise for themselves that there is a greater, nobler and more elastic role for them to play.

We are still dogged by the spectre of "part-time only and in the winter 9 p.m. to 5 a.m.," and still bound by the two-mile chain. We must throw these off.

Whilst the large majority must be local part-time soldiers, there are many of us who could become whole-time or periodically whole-time soldiers, and many who would willingly consent to being sent *wherever required*.

We should then have the beginnings of a mobile Home Guard Army on a practically professional footing and we should see in time H.G. units actually taking over from the Regulars, not only sedentary war duties but also mobile functions and duties of relief, whether temporary or permanent.

I dream of a day, not too distant, when the H.G. can say, "We are ready now to shoulder the principal burden of the land defence of these Islands, you Regulars can confidently leave it to us (as part of the Regular Defence—backed up and controlled by the Regulars) to enable you to go and make a job of it in the German-occupied countries, Germany, Italy or Africa or wherever you may be sent to finish this business once and for all."

I picture to myself intensified training during the winter on a far more ambitious scale, the doubling of the numbers of the H.G.—weapons or no weapons—the creation of a real General Staff involving the H.G., the acceptance of the principle that some of us can form a more elastic offensive-defensive force and the abolition of that beastly word "static."

Surely from the present strategical and administrative chrysalis will emerge a truly national army of H.G.

There is no magic wand that can transmute us into such an army—it requires knowledge, hard work, self-sacrifice, goodwill and guts—I do not think these qualities will be found wanting."

* * *

Was that true in 1940? Is it not true to-day?

A.F.U.G.

Storrington,
   October, 1942.

INDEX

Figures in *italics* indicate captions.

PICTURE CREDITS

Illustrations on the front endpapers taken from *Illustrated London News*, reproduced with permission of Mary Evans Picture Library/Illustrated London News Ltd.

Illustrations on the back endpapers taken from *Laughs With the Home Guard*, 1942.

All illustrations in the original pocket-book by A.F.U.G. Green.

Illustration on page 12, author's collection.

Image on page 17 reproduced with permission of Punch Ltd., www.punch.co.uk

" I want you men to imagine the enemy are approaching in large numbers,
supported by tanks, flamethrowers, paratroops, etc., etc . . . ''

[*The Venture*

Bank Manager : "Our cashier's just back from his Home Guard Training Course."